INSPIRING STORIES FOR AMAZING KIDS

(2 IN 1)

A Motivational Book for Boys & Girls about Courage, Perseverance, Problem-Solving and Friendship

Michelle Weiss

© 2024 Michelle Weiss

Cover and illustrations by: Jaime Suárez

All rights reserved.

No part of this publication may be reproduced, distributed, or transmitted in any form or by any means, including photocopying, recording, or other electronic or mechanical methods, without the prior written permission of the publisher, except as permitted by U.S. copyright law.

CONTENTS

BOOK 1

INSPIRING STORIES FOR AMAZING BOYS

INTRODUCTION 8

LIGHT THE LAMP 11

THE BIKE MAKER 21

YES, I'LL BE YOUR FRIEND 34

A LITTLE HELP IS ALL YOU NEED 44

ROAD TRIP 53

HELPING HAND 63

WORKING IT OUT 73

DANCING WITH TWO LEFT FEET 83

CURIOUS CURTIS 95

OLIVER'S PERSEVERANCE 104

EPILOGUE 116

BOOK 2

INSPIRING STORIES FOR AMAZING GIRLS

INTRODUCTION 119

STICKS AND STONES 121

CROSS MY HEART 134

SPREAD YOUR WINGS 145

NOTHING CAN STOP ME NOW 154

THE BIG SURPRISE 161

DON'T JUMP TO CONCLUSIONS 170

SYLVIA'S WISH 179

AVERIE'S PERSEVERANCE 189

PRACTICE MAKES PERFECT 199

A LISTENING EAR 210

EPILOGUE 219

JOIN OUR FACEBOOK GROUP!

If you want to:

- Discover the **latest releases**
- Be offered the possibility of **reading** every e-book (and for some lucky ones, the paperback!) **in advance for free**
- Share discussions with other members about the adventures and lessons your kids have found in our books
- **Learn about our books in progress** before anyone else, including illustrations, book covers, excerpts and more
- Receive some **free gifts**

And so much more!

Then join our Facebook community for exclusive access and fun surprises!

Scan this QR code to enter our group!

YOUR FREE GIFTS

As a way of saying thank you for your purchase, I'd like to offer you these two GIFTS, which I hope your child can enjoy!

To get access, go to the link or scan the QR:

https://michellebooks.com/free-gift

- The Amazing Coloring Book will set your little boy's creativity free!
- The Gratitude Journal will make him realize just how amazing his life truly is!

BOOK 1

INSPIRING STORIES FOR AMAZING BOYS

A Collection of Motivational Tales about Courage,

Perseverance, Problem-Solving and Friendship

INTRODUCTION

What if I told you, I could show you someone truly incredible? Well then, run as fast as you can. Find a mirror and look straight into it.

Yes, it's you!

You ARE incredible!

Yes, you heard that correctly! There's something clearly special about you. Something that makes you shine brighter than a star. No one, and I mean NO ONE, can ever be like you. You are unique. You are extraordinary. And that should make you feel proud of yourself.

Do you know what's even cooler? You can show everyone just how remarkable you are! You can light up a room with your smile. With your gentle heart, you can make a thousand friends. When you're yourself, you make magic happen.

Now, here's a little secret: Sometimes, shining like a star can be hard. Life can be difficult. But you know what? Even grown-ups face tough times! Just know that there's always a solution waiting to be found. And you know who finds those solutions? The ones who are patient and never give up – just like you!

You're not alone when you feel life is hard. In this book, you'll meet a bunch of new friends like you. They too sometimes find things a bit tricky. Some of them aren't good at making friends. Others feel a little shy. And some struggle with their grades. But you know what they do? They always face those challenges head-on.

As you read about them, you'll find new things too. Little treasures that you can use to become even more amazing. Each friend's story is like a magical treasure. And it's waiting for you to find and learn it.

Now I'm sure you're excited to meet all these new friends. But before I leave you, there's just one thing I want to say.

Always remember, dear boy, that I believe in you with all my heart. Keep being your wonderful self!

Your biggest fan,

Michelle

LIGHT THE LAMP

"Ryan, get a move on! You don't want to be late for the game!" Ryan's mom yelled up the stairs toward Ryan's room.

"Coming, Mom!" Ryan finished putting on his socks and grabbed his sneakers before running down the stairs. Ryan's hockey game was an hour from now, and he was energized and ready to play.

"We must make one stop on the way. Nikita needs a ride to the game."

Ryan stopped in his tracks. "What? Mom, you cannot give him a ride to the game! He hates me!" Ryan couldn't believe this was happening. He could feel the positive energy draining from his body, and his stomach tightened.

Nikita's mom and Ryan's mom worked at the school, and they became friends last year when Nikita and his mom moved into town. Nikita's mom was sweet and kind, not like Nikita. He was big, mean, and scary. No matter how hard he tried, Ryan had been unable to make friends with Nikita, despite being on the same hockey team for a half season, despite going to the same school, being the same age, and having the same awesome sport in common. Nikita refused to hang out with Ryan and told his mom he did not want to be friends. Nikita called Ryan names and made fun of his hockey skills. On the ice, Nikita was competitive and rough with Ryan.

Ryan's mom said Nikita was struggling to adjust to his new school. He was a big fish at his old school and was now a small fry. Whatever that meant.

"He does not hate you, honey," Ryan's mom said. "He is angry because he had to leave his school and friends behind to move here. Ryan, let's work together and help Nikita make friends. What do you say?"

"I want to get along with him, Mom. I would rather be friends with him because I see him everywhere I go. You don't understand. He won't let us be friends." Ryan was exhausted by the situation.

With Nikita on an opposing team this season, Ryan had come face-to-face with him in the locker room area before and after games and on the ice. Ryan and his teammates were always nice to Nikita and tried to talk with him about hockey or school, but Nikita wouldn't accept their kindness. He did not have friends on his own team.

As they pulled up to the house, Ryan saw Nikita sitting on the steps with his mother. Nikita was frowning and kicking his hockey bag with his foot.

Nikita's mom walked him to the car, and Ryan's stomach got tighter as Nikita got closer.

Nikita was taller than Ryan, and he had more muscle. Nikita was the biggest kid in school, and he looked even bigger when he put on his hockey equipment.

"Hey, Nikita. Ready for the game?" Ryan asked sheepishly.

"I am ready to watch you lose. That's for sure," Nikita grumbled as he looked out the window at his mother.

"Have a good game, honey." She kissed Nikita on the head. "Have a good game, Ryan."

"Thanks," Ryan replied and waved goodbye. Ryan wondered how such a mean boy came from such a nice woman.

Nikita stared hard out the window while Ryan tried to think of something to say. Before he could speak, his mother chimed in.

"There is no game next Saturday, not for either of you. The weather is getting nicer, and you two should ride bikes together. Or go to the park?" Ryan's mom looked back and forth from Ryan to Nikita.

"Do you have a bike, Nikita?" Ryan asked.

"Of course, I have a bike. I used to ride all the time with my friends back home. But we are not friends, and I'm not going to ride with you," Nikita replied nastily.

"I know some trails we could ride on," Ryan tried.

"Nope," Nikita stated firmly.

"I am sure you two could find something fun to do together. Nikita, I will let your mother know you will be coming over to our house on Saturday. I will feed you dinner also." Ryan looked at his mom and wondered if she would ever give up on the idea of him and Nikita being friends.

The rest of the car ride was silent.

On the ice, at the tail end of the third period, Ryan's team was down by one point. Ryan skated up center ice, head up, dribbling the puck side to side. His eyes scanned the area around him, looking for opportunities to pass the puck. The only thing Ryan could see was Nikita looming over the right side of the goal. Ryan's teammate Tomas was stuck behind Nikita, unable to break free and open himself for the pass. The team needed one more goal to win.

With no opportunity to the left of the goal, Ryan decided he would attempt to fake Nikita out. Faking out was something Ryan had been working on with his father. Ryan and his father loved to play hockey together. They played on the concrete floor in the garage, in the street, and throughout the house. All they needed were two sticks, a puck, and each other.

Nikita looked like a giant as Ryan skated directly at him. Ryan's knees felt weak. He was scared as Nikita skated faster toward him, and before he knew it, Nikita was inches from him, pushing his stick up in the air, forcing Ryan to lose control of the puck.

"Loser," Nikita laughed as he circled Ryan. Finally, the referee blew the whistle, and the players headed back to their bench.

"Good try, Ryan. Keep it up," Coach said.

"If I keep that up, we will lose for sure." Ryan sighed, disappointed in himself.

"Lean in and listen, kids." Coach grabbed his whiteboard, and the team gathered around.

"Ryan, I like that you tried to fake the other player out. I want you to do that again. I do not think he expects you to use the same move twice. Let's catch him by surprise."

"Tomas, I saw you trying your hardest to get out from behind that defenseman, Nick…Nikki. Whatever his name is."

"Nikita!" the whole team chimed in loudly.

"What I want you to do this time is, Tomas, when he blocks you, skate behind the goal. Come out on the left side. A fake out of your own. Nikita will not notice that you are no longer behind him because he will be focused on Ryan."

Coach continued, "Ryan, the fake out is that you will pass to Tomas instead of taking the shot yourself." Coach grinned from ear to ear, satisfied with his plan. Ryan and Tomas nodded in agreement with the plan as the rest of the team gave encouragement and patted them both on the helmet.

"It's worth a try, Tomas," Ryan said. "My dad says it is not about winning or losing, it's how you play the game. So, I'm going to play the best I can."

"Teamwork makes the dream work. That is what my dad says. But I still want to win." Tomas laughed and extended his gloved hand for a fist bump with Ryan. Returning the bump, Ryan laughed as he stepped back onto the ice.

Ryan wanted to celebrate the game-winning goal with Tomas. Tomas was a good friend and teammate, and he made Ryan feel good about himself. Ryan thought back to what Nikita said in the car about riding his bike with his friends. Ryan thought about how lonely he would be without Tomas and how lonely Nikita must feel without his friends.

On the ice, Ryan and Tomas worked together to execute the play as Coach had instructed. Ryan was able to fake Nikita out and pass the puck to Tomas. Tomas was able to sink the puck into the net. The team went wild when the red lamp behind the goal lit up. They had won by working together.

On the ride home, Ryan was excited about the win, smiling from ear to ear. Nikita looked unhappy as usual. Feeling good about the win and his friendship with his teammates, Ryan was determined to help Nikita make friends.

"We can eat your favorite food for supper on Saturday. What is your favorite food, Nikita?" Ryan asked.

Nikita hesitated. He looked at Ryan. He was not frowning anymore but not exactly smiling.

"Pepperoni pizza. I used to eat it with my friends all the time back home. I miss that." Nikita hung his head.

"Would you like it if I invited some of my teammates over for pizza? They all think you are a great hockey player, and I know they would like to get to know you more." Ryan waited, afraid that Nikita might not accept his offer.

"I would like that a lot. Eating pizza. And making new friends." At last, Nikita smiled. He held out his fist to Ryan for a fist bump.

"Sounds great, loser." Ryan returned the fist bump, and they both laughed heartily. Ryan smiled at his mom, proud of their work together to start this new friendship.

THE BIKE MAKER

Yuri hurried so he wouldn't have to pass Rusty, the meanest boy in the entire school. Yuri would ride his bike past Rusty each day, and Rusty would say mean things. Yuri ignored him and pedaled as fast as he could until he reached school.

"Hey, Yuri, where'd you get that piece of junk?" Rusty would shout. "Did you find that bike at the dump?" There was no end to Rusty's meanness. And it didn't stop once they reached school. Rusty would shoulder bump Yuri whenever he passed him in the hall.

One day, Rusty wasn't on the corner where he usually stood.

"Whew," Yuri said to his bike. "You won't get made fun of today."

Yuri safely reached school, and after putting his bike in the rack, he locked it. He was proud of his bicycle. It was a black bike with a red banana seat. It had silver metal petals and a silver kickstand.

He looked back at his bike as he opened the door. He couldn't wait for the day to be over so he could ride home without worrying about seeing Rusty. If Rusty wasn't on the corner, he probably wasn't at school.

And he wasn't.

The day was even better now that Rusty was absent. It was going to be the best sixth-grade day ever! Yuri was so happy. He hurried to the cafeteria to tell his friend Norah.

He found her sitting at their usual table.

"Why are you smiling like that, Yuri?" she asked. "Why are you so happy? Did you pass your math test?"

"Better than that," Yuri answered.

"Then what is it?"

"Oh, Norah, Rusty is absent today. I feel free! No bully to worry about."

"That's such good news, Yuri. But I hope he's not sick or hurt."

Yuri's smile faded. "Yeah, I thought of that. I just like not having to look over my shoulder all the time. I hope he's okay, though."

Norah nodded and took a bite of her sandwich.

Yuri knew she was right. No matter how badly Rusty treated him, wishing him harm wouldn't be right. Still, Yuri couldn't help feeling relieved that he could have a day without being bullied.

Norah and Yuri finished their lunches and walked to their music class. It was Yuri's favorite. He loved to sing and play the piano. His father worked hard to have the extra money for piano lessons.

Yuri felt so relaxed. He sang loud and proud. He went to his locker to put his books away when class ended. He put on his jacket and took the key to his bike lock out of the pocket.

"I'll see you tomorrow," Norah said as she passed him in the hall. "Maybe Rusty will be absent again."

Yuri smiled. "Maybe. We'll see. I'm just happy I got to enjoy today. See you tomorrow."

Yuri whistled as he walked to the bike rack. The air was warm, not too warm, just perfect for a slow bike ride home. He took a deep breath and rounded the corner to where his bike was waiting.

"Wh—what!" Yuri screamed. "Wh—wh—where's my bike?"

Yuri ran to the bike rack. His bike was gone.

He ran back inside the school and into the principal's office.

"Yuri, what's the matter?" the principal asked the crying boy. "Have a seat and tell me what happened."

"I don't want to sit. My bike is gone. It's gone!"

The principal stood. "I'm sure it's a mistake. Come, I'll walk with you to the bike rack."

"See, it's gone," Yuri cried as he pointed to where his bike once stood.

"Are you sure it was locked?" the principal asked.

"Pretty sure, sir. I don't think I forgot."

Yuri hung his head. His bike was gone. The principal took him back inside so he could call his mother to pick him up.

Yuri sobbed when his mother arrived. She hugged him and told him not to worry; he'd get another bike.

"I don't want another bike. I want that one. Dad made it for me."

"I know, son. And he will make you another. Now, come along. Let's go home and get you washed up for dinner."

Yuri wasn't hungry. He only wanted his bike.

"I'll make you another one just like it," his father said. "I'm sure I can find another banana seat."

Yuri looked at his father with a half-smile. No one would understand how much he wanted his bike back. The banana seat wasn't just any banana seat. It was given to him by his best friend, Jeff.

Yuri and Jeff had been friends since kindergarten. Jeff lived across the street from Yuri, and as they got older, they rode bikes together. Yuri admired Jeff's banana seat, and when Jeff had to move away to another city, he gave Yuri the seat.

"Take good care of it," Jeff had said as he hugged his friend goodbye.

It was a special seat, and Yuri knew his dad would never find another one.

Yuri's mother was clearing the dinner dishes when the doorbell rang. She opened the door to find Yuri's bike between Rusty and his mother.

"I am here to return your son's bicycle," Rusty's mother said. "And my son has something to say."

Rusty hung his head. "I'm sorry," he mumbled.

"Perhaps you need to say that to Yuri. Won't you come in? You can bring the bike in too. I'm going to put it in the kitchen. I'll be right back."

Yuri came down the stairs and was face to face with his worst nightmare—Rusty.

"What's he doing here, Mom?" Yuri asked.

Rusty's mother tugged his arm. "Don't you have something to say to Yuri?"

"Sorry I took your bike."

Yuri looked around. He didn't see his bike, so he was confused. Why was Rusty apologizing for taking his bike? He didn't bring it back.

"Yuri, go look in the kitchen," his mother said. "I think you'll be pleased."

Yuri ran to the kitchen and let out a screech. "My bike, my bike!" He ran back to the living room, where his mom, Rusty, and Rusty's mom sat.

"Thank you for bringing my bike back. But how did you take it? And why? And why do you bully me every day?"

Rusty's mother passed a stern look to her son. "You've been bullying Yuri? I think you need to explain yourself, and then we'll go home, and you can explain it to your father."

Rusty's eyes filled with tears, and he let out a whimper.

"I don't know why, Mom. I'm sorry. You and Dad can't afford to get me a bike. You said so yourself… because Dad's been sick and can't work. Yuri has a cool bike, and I guess I was jealous that he has a bike and friends. I don't have any friends."

Yuri walked over to Rusty and stood before him.

"You don't have friends because you scare everyone. You make us feel uncomfortable. You'd have lots of friends if you were nice."

"I'm sorry. I just wish I had a bike."

Yuri tapped Rusty on the shoulder. "Come with me," he urged.

The two boys went outside and walked to the large garage behind the house.

"Here, come on in," Yuri said. "I want you to meet my dad. He's known as the bike maker."

Rusty was surprised. "The bike maker?"

"Yes, my dad makes old bikes new again, and he donates them to kids who don't have bikes. Do you want my dad to make you a bike? You can pick the colors and the kind of seat you want. He'll do whatever you'd like."

"Really?" was all Rusty could say. He didn't understand how Yuri could be so nice to him after all he'd done. "Your dad will make me a bike?"

"I sure will, son," Yuri's dad said, and Rusty smiled ear to ear.

"I would really like that. Yuri, I'm going to cry. Are you going to tell everyone if I do?"

"No, it's okay to cry."

Rusty spent the next half hour picking out his bike. Yuri's dad promised to make it just the way he wanted it.

"Let's go back inside and tell our moms," Yuri said. "And by the way, how did you get my bike from the rack?"

"You didn't lock it," Rusty said. "I watched you from behind the tree. When you went inside, I took it and rode all day. I was going to bring it back, but I decided to keep it. That was stupid of me, I know. I didn't feel like going to school because my dad was sick all night. I just wanted to be alone. My mom doesn't know I skipped school yet. I guess I better tell her before the principal calls her tomorrow to ask why I wasn't there."

"It's okay, Rusty. I understand."

"You do? You aren't mad at me?"

"I'm not mad. But if you promise to stop bullying me, you can sit with Norah and me at lunch."

"Really?"

"Really."

"Let's shake on it," Rusty said and held out his hand.

The boys went inside to their waiting mothers.

"Meet my new friend Rusty," Yuri said proudly. "Dad is building him a custom bike, and when it's done, we'll ride to school together. And Rusty will sit with Norah and me at lunch every day."

"That's wonderful, dear," Yuri's mother said. "I'm happy you and Rusty can be friends. Let's go to the kitchen and celebrate with some ice cream. What do you say?"

Rusty noticed a piano in the family room as the foursome started for the kitchen.

"Wow! Who plays the piano? I've always wanted to play," he said excitedly.

"I play," Yuri said. "I take lessons. I can teach you if you'd like."

"Oh, boy, I sure would. You're the best friend ever, Yuri."

"Thanks, Rusty. I'm glad we are getting to know each other. Once you start being nice to everyone, you'll have a lot of friends. You'll see."

"Being nice makes everything better," Rusty said. "I'm not going to be mean to anyone ever again."

Three days later, Rusty's bike was ready, and together, he and Yuri rode to and from school, laughing and enjoying their new friendship.

YES, I'LL BE YOUR FRIEND

Toby sat in the school cafeteria alone. It was okay. He was used to it. You see, Toby was the only black student in the school. He didn't understand why no one would sit with him at lunch. They talked to him in class. They didn't pick on him or bully him. They just stayed away in the cafeteria.

Toby opened his lunchbox and took out his jelly sandwich. It was his favorite grape jelly on crustless bread. His mom took the crust off and made his sandwiches just how he liked them.

"Hey, Toby," Lizzy called to him halfway across the room. "How's your lunch?"

He didn't want to shout at her, so he smiled and nodded. "Why doesn't she just come over here to ask me?" he said under his breath. "She's kinda strange."

When the bell rang, Toby and his classmates lined up near the door, waiting for their teacher to come to get them.

Lizzy moved behind Toby.

"Hey, Toby, can I touch your hair?"

"Sure," he answered.

Lizzy liked to touch Toby's hair. She liked the texture and would often stand behind him in the lunch line so she could feel it.

Toby didn't mind. Sometimes the other kids would ask too. Toby knew his hair was different from his schoolmates, and that was okay. He liked who he was, and he enjoyed learning about his heritage. His mom told him always to be proud of who he was. His only wish was that he didn't have to sit alone at lunch.

Toby didn't say anything to his mom. He didn't want to worry her, and he didn't want his classmates to think he was whiny. He knew his mom would march down to the school to find out why her son was sitting alone in the cafeteria. Toby didn't want that at all. It wouldn't be cool.

He was afraid, too, that his mom would think it was because of his skin color. Toby knew better. That wasn't it. Still, he couldn't figure out why no one wanted to sit with or near him.

"Hey, Tobes," Josh called out from the front of the line. "Do you want to play with me at recess?"

"Sure," Toby replied, more confused than ever. Why, oh, why must he sit alone at lunch?

Toby had only been in the school for a month. He had to change schools when he and his mom had to move into a new house to be closer to his grandparents. His dad was in the Army and serving overseas, so Toby's mom thought it best to be close to her family.

Moving in the middle of the fourth grade wasn't fun for Toby. He had to leave his friends behind and make new ones. He was used to it, though. When his dad was stationed in the States, the family moved a lot.

Toby thought about the other schools he'd attended and how he never ate alone.

Making friends wasn't easy, but Lizzy and Josh seemed to like him. He thought they might want to be his friends someday.

As the class moved outside for recess, Josh ran over to Toby.

"Will you be my friend?" Josh asked.

Toby's eyes lit up, and his heart beat with excitement. "Yes, I'll be your friend."

"It's a deal," Josh said, offering his hand. "Friends, we are!"

"Great," Toby said. "Friends, we are!"

The two tossed a ball, and soon, Lizzy joined them.

They played three-way catch until the bell rang, signaling the time to return to class.

"We'll play again tomorrow," Josh said.

Toby couldn't wait. He had a new friend, and surely, Josh would sit with him at lunch.

He went home smiling from ear to ear. He knew he wouldn't be sitting alone in the cafeteria anymore.

The next day, Toby couldn't wait for lunchtime. He watched the clock, hoping that a lot of time had passed each time he looked.

It seemed to take forever, but finally, the lunch bell rang, and it was time to go to the cafeteria. Toby grabbed his lunchbox from the shelf and stood in line.

As they walked down the hall, Toby's excitement grew. He would soon be at a table with his new friend.

But—that didn't happen. Toby went to his usual seat, and Josh sat at a table with Lizzy and their friends.

Alone again, Toby was confused. He thought of asking Josh but didn't want to seem wimpy. He didn't want to invite himself to their table. They might not like that.

Sad, he faced the reality that his classmates, and even his new friend, didn't want to eat with a black kid.

That has to be it, he thought. *They don't want to eat with me because of my skin color.*

Why were they okay playing with him at recess and touching his hair? Why did Josh ask to be his friend? Don't friends sit together at lunch?

Toby finished his lunch and asked the lunch aide if he could be excused from the cafeteria. Then he went to the nurse's office and asked to lie down.

"What's wrong, Toby?" Nurse Andrews asked.

"My stomach aches," he answered.

Nurse Andrews told him to lie down while she called his mom.

"I'm okay now," he said. "You don't have to call my mom. She'll just worry over a little stomachache."

"Are you sure?" Nurse Andrews asked.

"I'm sure," Toby said. He got up and left.

The rest of the day went slowly, and finally, Toby was home.

"Young man, sit down. I need to speak to you," his mom said, pointing to the living room couch.

"Nurse Andrews called me this afternoon."

"It was just a stomachache, Mom. I ate too fast," Toby said.

"That's not why she called. She wanted to know why I hadn't sent in a doctor's note about your allergies."

Toby looked at his mom, confused. "What allergies?"

His mother gave her son a stern look. "That's exactly my question. Did you tell your teacher you have allergies?"

"No, Mom, why would I do that?"

His mother let out a loud sigh. "Then, why, son, are you sitting at the peanut allergy table in the cafeteria?"

"The what?" Toby asked.

"You heard me—the peanut allergy table in the cafeteria. You don't have peanut allergies. That table is for kids allergic to peanuts who need to sit away from the other kids. Nurse Andrews said you sit there every day and eat alone."

Toby laughed.

"What's so funny, son?"

"Oh, Mom, is that why no one will sit with me at lunch?"

"They can't, Toby. The school has special tables in the cafeteria for different food allergies. The other kids can't sit there because they could have something in their lunches that's harmful to those with food allergies."

Toby stood and danced around the room.

"Mom, I'm so happy! I can't wait to go to school tomorrow."

"Well, you'll have to wait, son."

Toby stopped dancing. "Why?"

"Because tomorrow's Saturday."

Toby laughed and danced his way to his bedroom. He was sure he had found the reason he was sitting alone.

Monday at school, when it was time for lunch, Toby sat at the table with Lizzy and Josh.

"Toby, what are you doing?" Josh asked. "You can't sit here."

"Why not?" Toby asked.

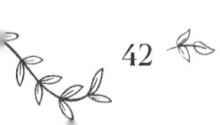

"I've got a peanut butter sandwich, that's why!" Josh shouted. "Do you want to get sick?"

Toby laughed. "I'm not allergic to peanuts or anything else. I didn't know that was the allergy table. Will you still be my friend?"

"Yes, I'll be your friend," Josh said as he scooched over. "Sit right here. It's where you'll sit from now on."

A LITTLE HELP IS ALL YOU NEED

The Weaver Middle School soccer team was on a winning streak. Antonio was giving his all this year, playing his best season yet. He felt happy and satisfied each time the team won, and his teammates would pat him on the back. On the field with his teammates was his favorite place to be.

Off the field, Antonio had different feelings. He did not like school. He especially didn't like homework. He often turned in assignments late or incomplete. He did not see the point in learning all the different subjects when all he wanted was to play soccer.

Coach Canton saw Antonio in the hall between classes and stopped him.

"Hey, Antonio! Bring your lunch to my office today. I need to talk to you about something important. See you at noon."

"No problem, Coach. See you at noon."

Antonio's mind went wild. He imagined all the compliments Coach was going to give him. He imagined Coach talking to him about being team captain next season.

At noon, Antonio carried his lunch tray to the athletics office and knocked on Coach's door.

"Come on in, Antonio. What's for lunch today?" Coach motioned to a small table and two chairs to the right of his desk.

"I got a salad and broccoli. Trying to eat healthily." Antonio hoped this would please Coach.

"Good thinking. Have a seat." Coach sat, taking out his lunch.

"What did you want to talk to me about?" Antonio pushed the broccoli around with his fork.

"Tony, I am so pleased with how you have been playing this season. I can see that you are making a one hundred percent effort on the field. You are applying what I teach you and working well with your teammates. So many others look up to your performance as something to strive toward."

Antonio smiled; his heart felt full.

"But... there is a problem with your performance in the classroom, Tony. Your grades are not as good as they need to be. As a member of the soccer team, you are required to maintain certain grades. And right now, Tony, you do not have those grades." Coach took a bite out of his sandwich and sat back in his chair. Antonio could not remember a time before when Coach had looked at him with disappointment. Antonio didn't like how it felt.

"You must sit out Friday's game. Tony, if your grades do not improve, you cannot continue with the team. It's not the school's rule. The state education department made the rule, and we must abide by it. Your grades need to improve, and fast."

"Coach, I'm sorry. I just…well…I don't like school, and I don't see why I need good grades to play sports."

"I didn't like school much when I was your age, but I loved sports, so I did what I had to do to play," Coach said.

Antonio didn't know what he'd do if he couldn't play. What would he do without his teammates? They were his friends.

He let out a long sigh. "Coach, I will do whatever it takes to stay on the team. I love it so much."

"I know a good tutor who can help you get your grades back on track. His name is Connor. You might know him; his locker is right next to yours."

"Connor Connolly?"

"Yes," Coach answered.

"But he's never said hi to me. Not once. Why would he want to tutor me when he's never spoken a word to me?"

"I've already spoken with him, and he's more than willing to help you with your schoolwork. Think it over, Antonio. I'd hate to lose you on the team."

Coach finished his sandwich. Antonio had lost his appetite and returned his tray to the cafeteria with the salad and the broccoli still on it.

At the end of the day, Antonio stood at his locker, putting his books away. Connor was at his locker, too.

"Hey, Antonio! Coach Canton asked if I could help you with your homework. What day can you meet with me in the library?"

"Why do you want to help me? You've never even said hi to me. Now, you want to help me get my grades up?" Antonio asked, looking Connor in the eyes.

"Hey, I'm sorry," Connor said sincerely. "It's just that you're a sports guy, and from what I've seen, an amazing one, and I'm a geek who no one really likes."

"Why would you say that? Do you think no one likes you? You seem like a cool dude."

"I don't have friends. Have you ever seen anyone hanging at my locker with me?" Connor shrugged his shoulders and closed his locker door. "Let me know what you decide."

"I'll tell you what, Connor. Let's meet in the library tomorrow after school, and you can help me. I have a game on Friday. If you can come, I'll introduce you to my teammates. They are all my friends, and they'll be happy to meet the dude who helps me stay on the team. What do you say?" Antonio asked, hopeful Connor would say yes.

And he did.

The following day, Antonio and Connor sat at the back table in the school library, working on math and science. They were the hardest subjects for Antonio. Somehow, Connor made it easy for Antonio to understand math problems.

"Wow, Connor. You really know how to explain math better than my teacher."

Connor laughed. "It's only because we are one-on-one and not in a room filled with other kids."

Friday came and after the soccer team's big win, Antonio found Connor in the grandstand and brought him to the field to meet the team.

"Hey, Connor, we're all going to Freddie's Restaurant across the street for fries and milkshakes. Can you come with us?" Antonio gave Connor a pleading look.

"Sure… I guess," Connor said. He had never been invited anywhere to be "one of the guys." He tried to hide his excitement.

"Wait here," Antonio said. "I've got to change in the locker room. I'll be right back. Don't go anywhere!"

Antonio's teammates welcomed Connor and invited him to sit with them in the cafeteria at lunch.

Not only did Connor and Antonio become best friends, but Antonio's grades also went up. He was passing everything and allowed to stay on the team.

Antonio got his report card and couldn't wait to show Connor.

"Look at this," Antonio said as they met at their lockers. "You really helped me a lot."

Connor smiled. "You helped me, too. I guess a little help is all we needed."

Antonio high-fived Connor. "Be at my game later."

Connor closed his locker and started walking away. "You bet I will."

ROAD TRIP

Manny looked at the clock. It was noon. He dreaded what was to come.

"Mom, do I have to go?" he whined. "Joey wants me to shoot hoops with him. Can I please do that instead?"

"I'm sorry, Manny. But you need to go with me."

Manny huffed and puffed as he walked to his mother's car. "This isn't fair," he mumbled under his breath. "A sunny Saturday afternoon, and I have to go with my mom."

As his mom drove, Manny sat in the back seat, pouting.

His mother looked at him in the rearview mirror. "You'd better have that look gone by the time we arrive," she said. "You have an hour left to change your attitude."

Manny rolled his eyes and checked his phone. His friends were all doing something fun—but not Manny. No, he had to travel with his mother to visit his grandfather. He hadn't met him before, at least not when he was old enough to remember.

His grandfather lived in California, and Manny and his parents lived in New York. Only a few weeks ago, Manny's grandfather moved to New York, just ninety minutes away. Now that he was so close, they'd be visiting more often, Manny's mother told him. He was not happy to hear that.

It wasn't only the long car ride that bothered Manny; it was missing his Saturday routine of being with his friends. He wanted to play basketball, baseball, or video games with them. Anything was better than visiting with someone he didn't know.

The ride seemed to take forever, and Manny was growing impatient. "Are we almost there, Mom? I mean, the sooner we get there, the sooner we leave, right?"

"We're about five minutes away, and no, we don't get to leave sooner. It doesn't work that way, Manny. This is my father, and I haven't seen him in three years."

"Oh, sorry."

"Someday, you'll understand. The last time I saw my dad was when you and I flew to California to see him. How would you like not seeing me or your father for three years?"

Manny wiggled in his seat. "Sorry, Mom. It's just that I'm eleven. I want to be with kids my age—my friends—and not many grown-ups."

"It will be fine, dear," his mother assured him. "We're here. Now, put a smile on your face, and let's go."

Manny slowly exited the car and walked to the door with his mother. She rang the bell, and an elderly man answered.

Manny watched as they hugged, and his mother cried. He stood back a bit to give them room.

"Oh, Dad," his mother cried. "Here's Emanuel. You haven't seen him since he was five. Look at how he's grown into a young man."

Manny offered his hand to his grandfather but was pulled into a hug. Unsure of what to do, he gave a slight return hug and said, "It's nice to meet you."

As they walked inside, Manny's grandfather said he wanted to hear all about Manny, his friends, and school.

"What would you like to call me?" his grandfather asked. "Grandpa? Elliott?"

"Your name is Elliott?" Manny asked, surprised. "That's such a cool name."

"Is that what you'd like to call me?"

"Sure."

Manny's mother shot a look of disapproval at them both. She didn't like the idea of her son disrespecting her father or any adult. She was raised to be respectful, and she was surprised her father made the offer to a twelve-year-old to refer to him by his first name, but she understood her dad was only trying to make Manny feel comfortable.

"Come to the kitchen," Elliott said. "I've got lunch waiting."

Manny hoped that once they ate, they could be on their way. Wasn't that what people usually did? Eat, talk for a few minutes, then leave? He was anxious to get home before dark to shoot some hoops with Joey. Maybe a game would be going on at the park by the time he got home. That's why Saturdays were so much fun. His mother didn't let him do much on Sundays. She said it was "family day." That's why he didn't understand why they made the trip on Saturday.

"When is Mom arriving?" Manny's mom asked her father.

"She's taking care of selling the rest of the furniture we don't need, then she'll be here. I hope it doesn't take much longer. I miss her being around."

"So do I, Dad."

Manny's mother and Elliott finished eating and sat talking. Elliott saw Manny was bored.

"Say, there, Emanuel, how would you like to come with me to see my special room?"

Manny's mother nodded. "That's a good idea, Dad. Did you get it set up here already?"

"Sure did. Come with me, Manny."

Elliott opened the door to a large room filled with all kinds of telescopes, space suits, and pictures. There was so much to see, Manny's jaw dropped.

"What is all this?" Manny asked as he wandered around the room.

"Manny, did your mother ever tell you what I did for a living?"

"No, why?"

"Have you learned about space in school?"

"Yeah, I have, but I've never looked through a telescope."

"Come spend the night sometime, and I'll show you the universe."

Manny's excitement grew. "I told my mom I want to be an astronaut someday," he said, pointing to a framed photo of an astronaut on a shelf.

"Well, it must run in the family. I'm happy you want to follow in my footsteps."

Manny turned to look at his grandfather. "What do you mean, follow in your footsteps?"

Elliott chuckled. "I'm an astronaut, son. I've been to the moon."

"What?! No way."

"Yes, way."

Manny walked around the room, looking at his grandfather's pictures and memorabilia. Even though his grandfather was young in the photos, he recognized him.

"This is the coolest ever!" Manny said as he stared at a picture of his grandfather as he boarded a spaceship.

"You… you're Elliott Stark! Wow. My class studied you. We learned all about you, and you're my… grandfather!"

Manny was so excited he could barely speak. "Can I… do you think… I would like…"

"What is it, son?"

Manny tried to talk, but no words would come out.

"Let's go back to the kitchen and get you something to drink."

Manny followed his grandfather to the kitchen, where his mother looked through photo albums.

"Mom, you… you never told me."

"I wanted my dad to tell you himself. What do you think?"

"I think it's the coolest. Do you think I could bring Joey the next time we come? Can we come next Saturday? How about tomorrow? It's Sunday. You said Sunday is family day."

"Slow down, Manny. We will be coming often, and you can ask your grandfather about bringing friends here."

"Can I, Grandpa? Can I?"

"Grandpa, hmm. I like the sound of that. Of course, bring all the friends you want. I have plenty of room here. Your grandmother wanted a big house, and she got one. The more, the merrier."

On the ride home, Manny talked nonstop about his grandfather. "How many kids in my school have a grandfather who's been to the moon? It's so cool, Mom."

His mother was happy for Manny, but she wanted to know something.

"Manny, what if Grandpa had been a plumber, accountant, or dentist?"

"He'd still be my grandpa, Mom. That's a silly question. He'd still be cool."

Manny's mother smiled. She wanted to be sure her son loved her father for who he was and not what he was.

"Grandpa is the best," Manny squealed. "He's been to the moon and can make a really good lunch. I can't wait to meet Grandma!"

HELPING HAND

Building a ramp would be difficult, but Milo was determined. Mrs. Waverly, Milo's neighbor, was generous to those around her, making baked goods for her neighbors and helping with their gardens. She had a big smile that rarely left her face. When Milo was in kindergarten, Mrs. Waverly would help him get on the bus when his mother had to go to work early in the morning. Each day, she would give Milo cookies to eat after he ate his lunch. She liked to tell stories of her career as an Army nurse, and Milo was fascinated by the tales of the places she had been. But now, Mrs. Waverly was older and had to use a walker to help her walk around. Sometimes, her son had to push her in a wheelchair.

One Sunday, Milo overheard his parents talking about building Mrs. Waverly a ramp so she could get in and out of her house more easily. He knew right away that he wanted to help.

Milo made a list of supplies he'd need and places he would need to go to get them. He told his parents about his plan, and his dad drove him around town to ask for donations.

Milo's first stop was Durk's lumberyard. His dad waited in the car while Mile went inside.

Milo walked over to the counter, where Mr. Durk was standing.

"What can I do for you, young man?" Mr. Durk asked.

"Hello, Mr. Durk. I don't know if you remember me. I'm Milo Stevens. My dad bought lumber from you last spring to build the shed in our backyard."

"I know your dad. I remember you, too. What is it you are looking for today?"

"My neighbor, Mrs. Waverly, has a tough time walking. It is hard for her to climb the stairs on her front porch. I want to build a ramp to make it easier for her, but I need lumber."

"Do you know how to build a ramp, son?" Mr. Durk questioned.

"No, but my dad does, and some of my neighbors," Milo answered nervously.

"Tell me when, where, and how much lumber you need, and I'll deliver it personally," Mr. Durk said, patting Milo on the back. "Have your dad call me with the measurements, and I'll even help you build the ramp."

Milo thanked Mr. Durk and ran to the car, excited to tell his dad.

"Now you have the lumber; what else do you need?"

"Dad, I think I'll need nails and a hammer. Maybe two hammers."

Milo's next stop was Clover Hardware. Destiny Clover had taken over the hardware store from her grandfather, and Milo knew she would be just the person to ask.

Milo burst through the storefront, excited to tell Destiny about his plans. She listened carefully as he explained why building a ramp for Mrs. Waverly was important.

"How could I say no, Milo? This is such a kind thing to do for Mrs. Waverly," Destiny said. "Do you know she used to babysit me? Of course, that was long ago, but I still remember what her house smelled like."

"Blueberry muffins," Milo and Destiny said in unison.

Destiny agreed to donate the hardware and let Milo borrow the tools he needed for the project.

"Thank you so much, Destiny," Milo said as he rushed to the car to tell his dad.

"What else do you need?" his dad asked.

"Nothing I can think of," Milo said.

"Are you sure about that?"

Milo thought for a few minutes as his dad waited for the silence to be broken.

"Son, do you think Mrs. Waverly would want to paint the railings to match the trim on her porch?"

Milo let out a deep breath.

"I almost forgot. We need paint!"

Milo continued his successful streak at the paint store. The owner generously donated a gift card for Mrs. Waverly to buy paint or stain when the ramp was complete.

As he returned home, Milo thought about Mrs. Waverly, her baked goods, and her garden. He was proud of what he had accomplished.

The only thing he needed to do was to find people to help build the ramp. Milo wanted to finish it in a day so Mrs. Waverly could get out if needed.

But how could Milo build a ramp in a day? He'd need a lot of help. He went to bed that night, tossing and turning, thinking of how to get others to help.

Then, like a lightbulb came on, he got an idea.

The next morning, he rushed to get dressed and ran out the door without eating breakfast.

"Milo," his mother called out, "Where are you going in such a hurry?"

"School, Mom. I've got a plan."

Milo huffed and puffed as he walked into the principal's office, catching his breath from his speed running.

"What is it, Milo?" Principal Anderson asked. "You look like a bear has chased you."

"Mr. Anderson, sir, I-I was wondering if I could put posters around the school?" he asked and explained why. "I need volunteers to help build the ramp."

"That's a great idea," Principal Anderson said. "I'll tell you what. I'll ask for volunteers when I make the morning announcements, and I'll stop by with pizza for you all to have for lunch that day."

"Wow," Milo said. "That's so awesome, Mr. Anderson."

"You're awesome," Mr. Anderson said. "You might not know this, but long before you were born, Mrs. Waverly was our school librarian. She was here for many years, even before I came here. You are a fine young man to do this for her."

Milo didn't need to hang any posters. Mr. Anderson's announcement and promise of pizza had volunteers lining up to join in.

Milo could hardly wait to see the smile on Mrs. Waverly's face.

He didn't need to wait long. The following Saturday, everyone showed up at Mrs. Waverly's house. The supplies were unloaded, and the volunteers were ready to get started. Even Mr. Anderson showed up in his work clothes.

They worked all morning, and Mr. Anderson left at noon to pick up the pizzas and juice.

The volunteers sat in the yard, eating and talking about how much they had already done. Mrs. Waverly called to Milo from the window.

"Come here. I have something for you," she said.

Milo walked to the open window, and Mrs. Waverly handed him the biggest plate of chocolate chip cookies he had ever seen."

"Thank you, thank you," he said. "They smell so good."

"They are fresh out of the oven," Mrs. Waverly said and winked.

Milo brought the cookies to the volunteers, and they were gone in minutes.

"Back to work," Milo's dad said. "Let's finish up this afternoon."

By five o'clock, the ramp was completed, and Mrs. Waverly stood in her doorway with tears welling in her eyes.

"I don't know what to say. The kindness you've shown me today and every day is overwhelming."

The volunteers clapped and cheered for Mrs. Waverly as she stepped out onto the ramp.

"It's so beautiful," she said. "You are truly remarkable," she said.

As the volunteers cleaned up the tools and prepared to leave, Mr. Anderson made an announcement.

"You students have shown that you will step up and answer the call of duty. Each of you will have a treat waiting in the office Monday morning. You'll all get a voucher to use at the school store."

Mr. Anderson's announcement was greeted with more cheering.

"This has been the best day ever," Milo said as he and his dad walked home.

"It sure was," his dad said. "And tomorrow, Mrs. Waverly's son will be painting the railings. I'm very proud of you, son. You are a fine young man, and you did something Mrs. Waverly will never forget."

"Thanks, Dad. But I just got it started. The rest was teamwork!"

WORKING IT OUT

My name is Manuel. My friends call me Manny. I am twelve years old and live in a town called Bath. It's a funny name, but it's a cool place. On one side of town is a river, and there's a forest on the other side. I live with my parents and annoying little sister on the forest side of town.

I have a best friend named Jordan. We are the same age and height, and he has an annoying little sister, too!

What's awesome is that we have more in common than annoying sisters. We both love to hike in the forest, look for wild mushrooms, identify animal tracks, and dip our feet into the stream to cool off on a hot day. Fishing in the river is another favorite thing of ours. It is a twenty-minute walk to the river, so we make a day of it. We pack lunch and drinks and make sure we have plenty of bait. We have been best friends for two years, and life has been great.

Life is still great. But I have one big problem. Things have changed between Jordan and me. Jordan is distracted and distant. He does not want to explore the forest or go fishing. We do not talk much these days either.

Want to know what changed it all?

Two words.

Cell phone.

Four months ago, we made plans for the spring hiking and fishing season, got our hiking gear in order, made sure our hiking boots still fit, and cleaned our backpacks for another year of exploring and working together to organize our tackle boxes and shovel snow to earn money for new fishing lures.

Then Jordan's parents gave him a cell phone. He was excited, and I was excited for him.

But slowly, the phone became his best friend. Jordan spent less time with me and more time with his phone.

Finally, one day, Jordan invited me to his house for a sleepover. I was happy that we were going to spend time together.

I packed my pajamas and toothbrush in my backpack, and my mom drove me to his house.

"Have a good time," she said when she dropped me off. "Call if you need me for anything."

I got out of the car with my backpack and a bag of snacks Mom made for us. Jordan was waiting for me by the door.

"Get in here," he said. "I can't wait to show you my new game!"

"Oh, we're going to play a game?" I asked. "What kind of game?"

"No, silly. Not you. Me. You can watch. It's a game on my phone. Only one can play."

We walked to his bedroom, and I sat on the edge of the bed next to Jordan.

"Watch this, Manny," he said as the screen jumped from scene to scene. I had no clue what I was supposed to be watching.

"This is kind of boring, Jordan. I have nothing to do."

"What do you mean, boring?" he asked curiously.

"I mean, you invited me here, and you're playing a game. I'm supposed just to sit here and watch?"

"Sure, why not?"

"Because it's boring."

Jordan said nothing and went back to his game. After an hour of doing nothing, I decided to go home. I asked Jordan's mom if she would call my mom to get me.

"Why, honey? Aren't you feeling well?" Jordan's mom asked me.

"I'm okay. It's just that there's nothing for me to do. Jordan's on his cell phone playing a game."

"He is? He's not supposed to be on that phone after five. It's almost seven o'clock. I'm going to have a word with him. Manny, please have a seat in the living room. I'll be back soon."

I waited on the couch in the living room like Jordan's mom told me to do. I just wanted to go home. I thought about leaving and walking home, but Mom wouldn't be too happy with me for walking alone when it was getting dark.

I'd rather be home with my annoying sister than here. If Jordan would rather be on his phone, I guess that's what he should do.

I don't want him to feel forced to do something with me. I wish he never got that stupid phone.

It seemed like forever before Jordan and his mom entered the living room.

"I'm sorry, Manny," Jordan said. "If you want to go home, that's okay."

"Excuse me, Jordan," his mom said. "It's not okay, and we agreed you would stay off the phone for the rest of the night, or I'll take it from you for a week."

"You can't do that, Mom!" You can't take it!" Jordan cried. "Manny can leave."

"Jordan, you invited him over, and now you're saying he can leave? Go to your room, and I'll be there shortly. I want you to think about what you just said."

I watched as Jordan stormed off. "Mrs. Smith, I'd like to go home. Can you please call my mom to pick me up?"

"I will, and I'm so sorry, Manny. I was wrong because I thought Jordan would be more responsible with a cell phone."

Days passed, and I didn't hear anything from Jordan. When I saw him at school, he wouldn't say hi, and he didn't sit with me at lunch like we used to. It didn't matter. Whenever I looked over to the table where he was sitting, he'd have his head down, looking at his phone.

I lost my best friend to a cell phone. I guess it's more fun than I was.

After another day of school without Jordan sitting with me at lunch, telling jokes, and making plans for fishing, I walked into the house to see Jordan's mom sitting at the kitchen table with my mom.

"Manny, Mrs. Smith would like to ask you a few questions," my mom said with a you-will-answer-them look.

I sat down, and Jordan's mom explained that the principal had called her because Jordan was on the phone during social studies class and refused to put it down when the teacher told him to.

"Can you tell me what happened in your own words," Jordan's mom asked.

"I'm sorry, Mrs. Smith. I don't have social studies with Jordan. We are only in lunch and gym together."

"Oh, I see," Jordan's mom looked confused. "I guess then... is there another Manny in your grade?"

"Not that I know of," I answered.

"Jordan told me you asked him to look something up for you on his phone, and that's why he was on it during class."

"Mrs. Smith, Jordan doesn't talk to me anymore since he got the phone. We don't sit in lunch together, and he doesn't say anything to me when I pass him in the hall."

"I-I don't know what to say. It appears Jordan has taken up lying. I need to go now. Thank you, Manny. You've been very helpful."

Wow. Jordan really isn't my best friend. He's not even a friend. He was blaming me when he got into trouble. Friends don't do that to friends.

After dinner, the doorbell rang, and Mom stood at the door talking to whoever it was while I put the dishes in the sink.

"Manny," she called from the living room. "Can you come in here?"

I went in, and Jordan and his mom stood there with Mom.

"Jordan has something to say to you," his mom said. "Go ahead, Jordan."

"I was wrong to be on the phone so much and ignore you. You're my best friend, and you're a lot more fun than a phone," Jordan said with his head down. "I'm sorry I lied about you to Mr. Lee, too."

I wasn't sure what to say.

Jordan lifted his head. "My mom said from now on, we need to solve our problems by talking things out. I know you weren't part of the problem, but I guess problem-solving is better than losing your best friend."

"Where's your phone?" I asked.

"In my mom's purse," he answered. "I can only use it for one hour after school and after I've done my homework. I don't want to use it more than that. I'd rather hang with my bestie."

"Can we hang, Mom?" I asked.

"If Mrs. Smith says it's okay."

Jordan's mom nodded, and my mom led her to the kitchen for pie and coffee.

"Let's go to my room!" I shouted to Jordan. "The last one there is a rotten egg!"

Jordan took off toward my room, laughing. I ran after him as fast as I could, happy we were friends again.

DANCING WITH TWO LEFT FEET

It was almost time for the Nelson Junior High School's annual Valentine's dance. It was one of the most exciting times of the year as the dance was different from most of the school's dances—the Valentine dance meant girls asked the boys. The entire school could attend, even the kindergarteners.

The younger kids could ask their dads, brothers, or uncles. The older kids, like Harry, had to be asked by a girl.

And Harry wanted nothing more than to go to the dance with Mandy. He was certain she wouldn't ask him. After all, Mandy was pretty and popular, and Harry was nerdy. Some kids called him "pocket calculator" because he was smart and always at the top of his class.

"No girl will ask me to the Valentine's Day dance," he told his best friend Claude during lunch. "Especially Mandy. She'd never ask me."

"You don't know that, Harry. You need more self-confidence," Claude said.

Harry sighed. "Well, Anna Marie asked you, so you have a date. I'll be the only boy in the school not invited to the dance."

Claude shook his head. "Harry, I can tell Mandy you'd be interested in going with her."

Harry sprang to his feet. "Don't you dare! I would be so embarrassed if you did that. I'll look desperate."

Claude shrugged and sat eating as Harry walked off. He knew it was useless to convince Harry that he was not as unpopular as he thought.

Harry hurried to his locker, hoping he could avoid Mandy. He was worried because Mandy's locker was next to the door to the science room—Harry's next class.

"Hey, Harry!"

Oh, no. The plan to avoid Mandy didn't work. He gave her a nod and rushed into science class.

"How will she ever ask you to the dance if you keep running away from her?" Claude asked as he came up behind Harry.

"She's not going to ask me, and besides, I have two left feet. I can't dance. I look silly when I even try. Why do you think my little sister hasn't asked me to take her? She's going with our dad."

"She probably wants to go with your dad, and I doubt Sally cares how you dance. She's six!"

"Claude, Sally laughed at me all night when I danced at our Uncle Immal's wedding. Then, she teased me when we got home. No, thank you. I am not going to ask anyone to the dance."

"Anna Marie will teach you how to dance," Claude said. "You need to stop making excuses and take some lessons."

Harry took his seat. He wasn't going to take dance lessons, and even if he were the best dancer in the school, Mandy wouldn't go anywhere with the pocket calculator kid.

Harry stopped paying attention to his science teacher and daydreamed about dancing with Mandy. He pictured himself as an amazing dancer who could draw a crowd as he swung his partner around and around.

"Harry… Harry, are you paying attention?" Mr. Southworth asked.

"I, um, well, what's the question?"

The bell saved Harry. He jumped up as it rang and rushed to avoid Mandy.

It didn't work.

"Harry," Mandy called out, "why are you always avoiding me? I don't bite."

Yes, you do, Harry thought, but instead, he turned to her and said, "I can't be late for math."

"Harry Carpenter, you are always avoiding me. I need to ask you something, but you keep running away."

Oh, no. Here it comes. Harry had prepared his answer to decline any invitations to the Valentine's Day dance, and he was about to put it to use.

"What is it?" he asked shyly, ready to give his short speech about how he made plans before he realized it was the same date as the dance.

"Harry, would you… I mean, oh, well, I'll just come right out and ask."

He interrupted, "Mandy, it's okay. You don't need to be scared to ask. The answer is, I'm sorry, but I can't go to the dance with you. I made plans before I knew it was…"

Harry didn't get to finish his sentence because Mandy burst out laughing. "No, silly. I'm not asking you to the dance. I've already asked Michael. Did you really think I'd ask you to go to a dance with me?"

"Well, I—"

"I wanted to ask if you would write a book report for me. I don't want to read the book, and I really need an "A," or my mom and dad will ground me, and I won't be able to go to the dance. I can pay you five dollars."

"Sorry, Mandy. I'm not for sale, and sorry about the mix-up."

Harry rushed off, his face hot and flushed. He wanted to cry. He was so embarrassed. What made him think a girl like Mandy would ask him to the Valentine's dance or any dance?

He saw Claude coming in the opposite direction and tried to speed up so he could duck into the library, but it was too late.

"Dude, what's wrong? You look like you're going to cry, and your face is beet red. You okay?"

"Sure, Claude. I'm fine," Harry answered, his voice cracking.

Claude pulled Harry by the arm. "We're going to talk about this after school. Don't leave without me."

Harry and Claude always walked to and from school together every day. Claude lived two houses away from Harry. They hung out often, and Harry liked Anna Marie even when she interrupted whatever he and Claude were doing.

As they walked home, Harry told Claude everything.

"You're kidding, right? She wanted to pay you to do her homework? A girl like that isn't worth breaking a sweat over. I think you need to forget her. You've crushed on her long enough, and you need to move on."

"She's going to the dance with Michael," Harry said. "She was proud to tell me that."

"Harry, you're going to the dance. I know a friend of Anna Marie's who would love to go with you."

"Who would that be?" Harry asked curiously.

"Demi Fish."

Harry laughed. "Demi Fish? But she can barely speak English."

Claude gave Harry a pat on the back. "Harry, she's a nice girl, and she's been working on her English."

"I'll think about it," Harry said and went inside his house.

He thought Demi Fish was kind of cute, and she smiled a lot, which Harry thought was nice.

After dinner, the doorbell rang. Harry's mom answered.

"Harry, there's someone here to see you," his mother called. "She's in the living room."

She? Who could "she" be? He rushed to the living room to find Mandy sitting with her hands folded in her lap.

"What are you doing here, Mandy? I told you I'm not going to write your book report."

"I know. I came to apologize for asking you to do it and, worse, offering you money. It was wrong, and I'm sorry."

Harry stood, not saying anything but looking Mandy straight in the eyes. "I accept your apology and appreciate that you know it was wrong to ask."

"Thank you, Harry. I was wondering if you'd like to go to the May dance with me?"

Harry was taken by surprise.

"Um, thank you for asking, but no, I have a date. At least, I think I do. Besides, I thought you were going with Michael?"

"I was, but he got the flu."

"I'm not interested in playing second fiddle, but I hope you find a date."

"Thanks, Harry. Again, I'm sorry, and I hope we can be friends." Mandy offered her hand.

"We can be friends," Harry said as they shook. "Come on. I'll walk you out."

Harry said goodbye to Mandy and walked to Claude's house.

"You won't believe this," Harry said. "Mandy came over to apologize and ask me to the dance. I said no, of course."

"Good," a voice from another room called out. "Because I want to ask you."

Demi walked into the room with Anna Marie.

"Demi and Anna Marie are giving me dance lessons," Claude said. "You see, I'm like you. I have two left feet, but that won't keep me from the dance. I don't care what others think of me, and neither should you,"

"Demi, I would love to go with you, but I can't dance at all," Harry said.

"No, no, that's okay. I don't speak English well. So we are… what do you call it? Even?"

Harry laughed. "Even."

The four spent the rest of the evening working on their dance moves. By the night of the dance, Harry was confident he no longer had two left feet.

"Wow, you look beautiful," he said when he picked up Demi to take her to the dance.

As they walked to Harry's mom's car, he gave Claude a thumbs-up. Not only was Harry ready to dance the night away, Demi looked beautiful.

Harry took her hand. "I might not understand everything you say, so please don't get mad, okay?"

Demi smiled. "I won't get mad, Harry. Dancing is a universal language. That is how we can communicate with people all over the world."

Harry couldn't agree more.

CURIOUS CURTIS

Curtis was a curious child. Even when he was a toddler, he explored everything around him. He would pick up bugs and want to know everything about them. When his sister was born, he would look at her for hours, asking his mother questions.

"Why can't she talk?"

"Why does she sleep so much?"

"Why can't she walk?"

"When can she play with me?"

As Curtis got older and started school, he would ask his teachers many questions. Sometimes, his curiosity would cause him to interrupt the lesson to ask something.

When Curtis was in third grade, his teacher, Mrs. McGrath, had no patience with his constant questioning. She sent a note home to Curtis' parents, asking them to teach him better manners so he wasn't interrupting her lessons.

"Please have Curtis understand that I need to teach the entire class and can't be stopping every few minutes to answer his questions," Mrs. McGrath wrote. "He asks questions that are answered as I proceed with the lesson. All he needs to do is wait for me to finish. His questions would then be answered."

Curtis' mother knew of her son's curious nature and inquisitive mind. She had tried everything to get him to stop asking so many questions. She didn't want him to stop completely, but she did want him to slow down at least.

"Curtis, you need to stop interrupting your teachers," his mother told him after reading Mrs. McGrath's note. "You need to let Mrs. McGrath finish her lessons. Then, if you still have questions, you can ask."

"Why?" Curtis asked.

"Why? Because it's not fair to your classmates," his mother answered.

"Why?" Curtis asked again.

"Curtis, we have gone over this many times. You cannot question everything. You need to be respectful of others."

Curtis sighed. "May I go to my room?"

"You may," his mother said. "I will call you when dinner's ready."

Curtis sat at his desk reading an encyclopedia. He liked to read about different people and species of wildlife. When no one would answer his questions, an encyclopedia would. He could let his imagination take him anywhere without his parents' permission. He was happy when he didn't have to ask questions to know more.

Curtis stopped asking so many questions in class; on some days, he didn't ask any questions.

But when he stopped asking questions, his grades started to slide. And that meant another note home from Mrs. McGrath.

"Curtis is no longer interrupting my lessons. In fact, he doesn't seem to pay attention, and his grades are slipping. His English grade has fallen from one hundred to ninety-two, and his reading grade has dropped from ninety-nine to ninety. Although his grades are still high, Curtis is not putting out the quality of work he has been doing. I am concerned his grades will continue to drop without intervention."

Curtis' mom knew she had to do something. Curtis was a smart boy, and he loved school and learning. She didn't understand why he would let his grades slip.

"Curtis, what's going on with you?" she asked him at the dinner table.

"Yes, son, I would like to know, too," his father said.

"Nothing," Curtis answered, not looking up from his plate as he pushed his vegetables around. "Things got harder, that's all."

"Very well," his father said. "We don't expect you always to get perfect grades, but we become concerned when your teacher tells us your grades suddenly dropped."

"Yes, Dad. I'll try to do better," Curtis answered.

"That's all your mother and I expect," his dad said. "Now, how about eating some of those peas instead of pushing them back and forth on your plate."

"Sure, Dad," Curtis answered, taking a spoonful of peas. They were his favorite vegetable.

"Oh, and I almost forgot," his mother said, "your grandfather will pick you up from school tomorrow, and you can spend the weekend with him. Pack what you need tonight, and I'll drop it off to Grandpa after I drop you off at school."

Curtis was excited about spending the weekend with his grandfather. He could ask all the questions he wanted, and his grandfather would answer. No one told him he was interrupting or shouldn't be asking so many questions. He could be himself around his grandpa.

The next morning, Curtis kissed his mother on the cheek and got out of the car. He spent the day not saying anything in class. He did his work, got a perfect score on his math test, and helped a classmate with a science problem. Finally, the bell rang, and Curtis ran to his grandfather's car.

"Let's stop for ice cream," his grandfather said. "Don't you think it's a great day for a large vanilla sprinkle cone?"

"Yes! Curtis was excited. That's one thing he loved about going to his grandfather's. They had ice cream a lot. Curtis knew how much his grandfather loved to eat ice cream, so he never said no. He knew he'd be eating a lot of ice cream all weekend.

When they arrived home from the ice cream stand, Grandpa led Curtis into the house and his den, where he built a hotel model.

"You're the best architect in the world," Curtis said, admiring his model.

Grandpa laughed. "I'm the only architect, you know!"

Curtis asked questions about the hotel, and his grandfather answered each.

Then, Curtis became quiet, and his grandfather asked why.

Curtis explained everything—what his teacher said, the notes home, his slipping grades, and how he can't help but want to know everything there is to know.

"Son, I understand you want to know everything, but the world is large, and it's impossible to know everything. That's why we have careers."

"Careers?" Curtis asked.

"Yes, careers. They are jobs you have for a long time. Take me, for instance. My career is as an architect. Your dad is an accountant. Your mom doesn't work right now, but she was a school principal before you were born."

"I'm sure glad she isn't a school principal anymore. I wouldn't want to be sent to her office!"

Grandpa laughed. "There are plenty of careers for curious boys and girls. Curious people become news reporters, detectives, anthropologists, and geologists. If your curiosity is about animals and how they interact with one another, a zoologist is a perfect career. You'll find the perfect career for your curious mind when you get older."

"Thank you, Grandpa. Do you mind if I ask you questions about curious careers?"

"Not at all, son. Not at all."

OLIVER'S PERSEVERANCE

Smack! Smack!

A pair of two little feet slapped against the floor.

Delilah sighed as she passed the oil to her mom, "Here he comes…"

The kitchen door swung open.

"I want pizza now!" Oliver exclaimed, frustrated.

Delilah rolled her eyes, and Mom offered a soft smile.

"I'm kneading the dough now, honey," Mom said as she folded and punched the dough. "You know, good things take time."

Oliver's pout deepened. He certainly did not like good things to take time. They did not just take time. They took *too* much time.

He folded his arms across his chest. "But waiting is so hard!"

He huffed loudly and stomped out of the kitchen. The pizza took another two hours to reach the dining table. Even though it did taste amazing, Oliver wished it had taken less time.

"Mmmmhhhh... why did you take so long to get ready," Oliver mumbled as he bit into his slice.

Later that week, Oliver was stuck on a test at school. He looked at his worksheet. Only two out of the ten questions had been answered.

"Ughhhh!" Oliver groaned. It felt like all the numbers were wiggling on the page like ants.

Oliver's brow furrowed. His pencil tapped against the desk.

"Why is this test taking so long?!" he mumbled in frustration.

It wasn't as though Oliver didn't know the test. He had studied for it. He knew how to answer the questions. In his mind, it just took too long to write it all, to solve everything.

Tik, tok, tik, tok.

The time passed quickly.

"That's it!" Oliver said. "I give up!"

He simply could not work his brain harder. It took too long to answer the questions. He picked up his worksheet and stomped to the teacher's desk.

"Are you done?" Ms. Johnson asked as Oliver pushed his test toward her.

She frowned as she unfolded the page and saw eight unanswered questions.

"I'm done," Oliver replied, tapping his foot.

"A good grade doesn't come without hard work, right?" Ms. Johnson pointed out.

"I'm done," Oliver repeated, not looking at his teacher.

He didn't understand adults. Why did they like for things to be slow? Why did they not want everything to happen quickly?

Soon, the bell rang, signalling the end of the school day. Oliver ran and hopped into his mom's car. She was going to take him to his piano class.

"Vroom! Vroom!" The entire way, Oliver imagined he was in a sports car. He sped down the road. A sharp cut and he drifted at the turn. Within seconds, he had reached his destination.

"We're here, Oliver!" his mom announced.

Oliver kissed his mom goodbye and ran to his class. The fleeting time of speeding was gone. Oliver felt he was back in slow motion.

He stood before the piano, its keys gleaming. He played a few notes.

"Ding, ding, ding!"

The music sounded like magic to his ears. Yet, this was all he could do: play random notes. He didn't know how to play an actual song.

Again, there was only one problem. The only problem Oliver had was with everything. Practicing and learning took too much time.

"I'm tired…" Oliver sighed. "I don't have time to practice. I just want to play and make magic happen!"

He had been taking lessons with Mr. Henry for days now. Yet, he couldn't get past the first stanza. Even with that, he made many mistakes. Oliver wished his fingers could create music.

"Oliver, again!" Mr. Henry said sharply. "You know, practice makes perfect."

Oliver sighed deeply. Same old words. Words he did not understand. Yet, he returned his fingers to the piano as Mr. Henry had instructed.

That weekend, the weather was perfect.

"Why don't we go to the beach today?" Oliver's dad asked as he peeked through the curtains early in the morning. And that's how the entire family ended up at the beach.

The sand stretched out as far as Oliver could see. The waves clashed like warriors. Oliver sat to watch this amazing fight. But then, he had another idea. The winning warrior would need a place—a castle, to be exact.

Oliver looked at the sand and the bucket and shovel he had brought. His eyes sparkled with an idea.

Oliver grabbed hold of his toys and started filling the bucket with sand. He pressed the sand into the bucket. He then turned it over to create the base of the castle. He worked hard at it, but suddenly, one side of his castle fell.

"Noooooo!" Oliver cried. He had put so much work into the castle. But now it was ruined.

"I give up…"

Oliver was so angry that he was about to throw his shovel into the sea. That's when he heard another voice.

"Hahahaha!" Oliver looked up to see a girl his age sitting nearby. She was pointing at his ruined castle and laughing loudly. "Awww, you poor baby."

Baby?

Baby!

The word made Oliver angrier than before.

"My castle is perfect." The girl flipped her ponytail proudly.

That was it. The girl had awakened the monster inside Oliver.

"I can make an even better one," Oliver said.

The competition started. Oliver forgot about his first failed attempt and started working on his new castle. His castle did fall many times. Yet, not once did he give up. Oliver had only one thing on his mind. He had to make a castle better than the girl's.

"No," Oliver muttered. "My castle will be better than every kid's castle on this beach!"

Scoop! Pat! Pat!

Oliver worked tirelessly. His hands moved quickly. The sand began to take shape slowly. It grew bigger and bigger.

"Take that!" Oliver grinned, sticking a seashell flag on his castle. He was going to show everyone how great his castle was.

Just as Oliver was about to finish his castle, something happened again. Suddenly, a huge wave crashed into the beach.

SPLASH!!!

Oliver's castle was awfully close to the beach. And so, it was knocked over.

"Ahh!" Oliver shouted but stopped as soon as he saw the girl. Once again, she was laughing at him. Yet, this time, she was joined by another boy. He was trying to make a castle as well.

Seeing their smug faces, Oliver knew only one thing. He was not going to give up. He was going to work even harder. He was going to start over yet again.

"I won't let you guys' win!" Oliver muttered under his breath.

He began building. First, the castle's base and then the walls. Slowly, he put it all together again. It truly was the most giant castle he had ever tried to make.

"I'll show them all!" he thought, filling his bucket with sand.

With a proud smile, Oliver finally finished his sand castle just as his mom walked by.

"Oh my, Oliver!" she said in amazement. "Did you make that?"

"Yes!" Oliver nodded. "I'm in a race."

"Well, I don't know about any race, honey." his mom replied. "But I do see an amazing castle."

"Is it?" Oliver asked, shocked. He looked at his castle again as though for the first time.

"Yes, it's incredible!" his mom replied, excitedly.

Oliver grinned from ear to ear. His castle was bigger than everyone's on the beach. It was also the most beautiful castle he had ever made.

Oliver's mom gathered the entire family to take pictures around his castle. Yet, the whole time Oliver's eyes stayed on his creation. He realized how much time and hard work it took to make the castle fantastic. Yes, there were failures, too. But each failure had taught him something, and each time, he learned how to make his castle even better.

It was the first time in his life he understood the grownups. They were right when they said good things could take time. All he had to do was not give up. And he could do anything he put his mind to.

Things changed from that day. Oliver understood the importance of patience. He knew how important it was to wait for the right time. Yet, while he waited, he also had to work hard for what he wanted and never give up.

In school, Oliver gave proper time to all his tests. He carefully answered all the questions. He knew getting a good grade was not going to be easy.

During his piano lessons, he worked harder. With Mr. Henry, Oliver practiced for hours on end. He recalled how his castle took many tries to build. Just like that, every mistake in his piano lessons helped him get better. And one day, he was going to become the best pianist.

Until then, Oliver was going to keep on working hard. He would never give up because slow and steady wins the race.

EPILOGUE

And I'm back!

You did it. You've reached the end (almost). But a celebration is definitely in order. I'm proud of you!

Between these pages, you went on a journey with your new friends. How fantastic is that? You've learned so much from them. And along the way, you've become even more wonderful.

Remember, just like your new friends, you can do anything. Toby learned to make friends even when it seemed a bit tricky. Antonio found out it's okay to ask for help and get better. Manny understood how all grandparents should be loved and respected. Milo showed how rewarding helping others can be. Manuel thinks smart and solves everything. While Harry finally finds the courage hidden deep inside of him. So, if you are ever faced with something tough, don't worry! You're a super problem-solver, just like all your new mates.

Remember, keep being the incredible person you are. Spread your magic, just like your friends did in their stories. And you know what? Maybe someday, your own amazing story will be in a book too.

Till then, never forget how special you are. You have made me your fan already. I bet you will make many more.

So, keep being you, dude!

High-fives and fist-bumps,

Michelle

BOOK 2

INSPIRING STORIES FOR AMAZING GIRLS

A Motivational & Empowering Book about Courage,

Perseverance, Problem-Solving and Friendship

INTRODUCTION

What if I could show you the poster girl for strength?

It's time to flip that front camera open and meet the most confident girl I know.

It's you, my dear.

You probably don't believe me right now, but I know the beautiful, bold girl inside you. This is exactly where we (me and all the girls you'll meet inside this book) come in.

Welcome to an entirely new magical world. A world where brave, kind and intelligent young women like you weave their life stories. These girls have brought to you this collection of short stories to not only entertain you but to inspire you as well. To remind you that you are a strong, confident and incredible girl who can do anything in this life.

As you read on and meet each new girl, you'll see they aren't princesses living in castles. They are heroes who face challenges just like you do. And they are here to show you how like them, you can make your dreams come true.

Hidden between the pages of this book are gems of possibility and diamonds of confidence. They shimmer in the darkest of times and the faintest of light. A constant reminder that you have everything it takes to bring your dreams to life. You can do anything you put your mind to, no matter what.

So, my dear girl, get ready to discover how you can change the ordinary into the extraordinary and flip challenges into opportunities. And throughout it all, I hope you learn only one thing: that you are the most unique and incredible thing on this earth.

With a huge hug and lots of well wishes,

Michelle

STICKS AND STONES

Jimmy was bored. It was Saturday morning, and the July sun was warm and bright. He looked out his bedroom window, but none of the neighborhood kids were around—none, that is, except for Gina. Jimmy liked Gina, but sometimes she was too goody-two-shoes.

Jimmy yawned and walked across the street to see if Gina wanted to play. She was sitting on her porch steps when he approached.

"Hey there, Gina. Do you want to play something?"

"Sure. What?" she said, excited to have someone to play with.

"Dunno." Jimmy shrugged. "We could play catch."

"Great!" Gina jumped up and went into her house to grab a ball. She was happy to have someone to play with too. As the youngest child in the neighborhood, sometimes some of the other kids didn't want her around.

"Go home," they'd say. "You're too little."

"But I'm nine," she'd reply. "I am old enough to play."

It didn't matter what she said or how much she pleaded, they wouldn't let her play.

Jimmy was eleven and sometimes got into trouble for doing silly things. One day, he picked flowers from Mrs. Finch's garden to give to his teacher, and Mrs. Finch was so mad she made Jimmy plant her new flowers.

Jimmy stood when Gina came back outside with a ball.

"Let's go to the backyard," she said. "We'll have lots of room."

Jimmy and Gina tossed the ball back and forth in Gina's backyard for fifteen minutes when Jimmy got bored again.

"I don't want to do this anymore. Let's think of something else," he said. Just then, he spotted a small pile of white stones. "Hey, Gina," he said, pointing. "What are those stones for?"

"Oh, those are for my mom's garden. She plants her flowers and puts them on top of the soil. I guess to look pretty. Those are the leftovers."

"Hmm," Jimmy said. "Did you notice Mrs. O'Connor isn't home? She's probably gone for the day to visit her husband. My mom said he's in a nursing home."

"I know. I miss Mr. O'Connor. I saw him the day Mrs. O'Connor had to take him to the home. He looked so sad."

Jimmy and Gina sat on the lawn, thinking about what to do next. They didn't want to waste a sunny day, but they didn't have many options with no one else around.

Suddenly, Jimmy jumped up. "I've got an idea! Let's throw the stones near Mrs. O'Connor's dog and see if we can make him bark."

Gina stood. "Why would we want to do that? It sounds mean."

"Oh, come on. It will be fun. Those stones are small, and we won't hit him. Let's just make him bark."

"That's not fun, Jimmy. And it's not right."

Gina knew Mrs. O'Connor only tied her dog Smokey outside when she was going to be gone all day. Smokey was a good dog, and he loved kids. Sometimes Mrs. O'Connor would let Gina bring Smokey next door to her house.

Jimmy walked over to the stone pile. "I'll just throw a couple to see if he'll bark."

"No, Jimmy. Don't. It's not a good idea. My mom and dad won't like it, and Mrs. O'Connor won't like it."

"Don't be a baby. I'll just toss a few, and then I'll go over and pick them up."

"But—" Gina sat back down and shook her head. She knew nothing she said would change Jimmy's mind.

The O'Connors were the best next-door neighbors anyone could ask for. Gina liked to help Mrs. O'Connor carry in her groceries, and sometimes she would take Smokey for walks around the block.

"Hey, look," Jimmy called out, holding some small sticks. "I'll toss these near the dog too. Maybe he'll pick them up with his mouth and chew them or move them. Maybe he'll build something." Jimmy laughed.

"Stop it," Gina said, her blonde ponytail swaying as she shook her head. "You leave Smokey alone. Let's go do something else."

"Nope. I'll throw the sticks and stones until that stupid dog barks."

"Why? He's a good dog. Why don't you go home now," Gina urged.

"Nope. And if you want to ever play with me or anyone again, you'll keep your mouth shut."

Gina dropped her head, and a tear rolled down her cheek as Jimmy threw sticks and stones at the neighbor's side yard.

Before long, Jimmy had tossed almost all the stones. Gina knew her mom would be mad.

"Aren't you going to pick them up?" Gina asked Jimmy.

"Nope."

Just then, Mrs. O'Connor returned. She got out of her car and looked at all the sticks and stones near Smokey.

"I'm out of here, Gina. Don't tattle on me, or I'll tell everyone you're a baby tattletale. You gotta protect me."

Jimmy ran home so fast that Gina didn't have a chance to say anything. She went into her house, hoping Mrs. O'Connor wouldn't know how the stones got in her yard.

At dinner, Gina could only pick at her food. She wanted to tell her mom and dad about Jimmy and what happened, but she was too scared. She didn't want to be known as a tattletale and wanted to have friends. She couldn't think about what her life would be like with no one to play with.

"You're not eating much," Gina's mother said with concern. "Are you feeling okay?"

"Yes, Mom. I'm fine. I'm just not too hungry."

"You don't have to eat. You may be excused."

Gina left the table and went to her bedroom. She thought about Jimmy and was mad at herself for not stopping him.

As she stared out the window, her thoughts were interrupted when the doorbell rang. She listened as her mom and another woman spoke. Suddenly, she recognized the voice.

It was Mrs. O'Connor.

"Gina, will you come down here, please," her mother called from the bottom of the staircase.

"Yes, Mom," Gina answered. She walked slowly down the stairs as her mom stood waiting.

"Gina, Mrs. O'Connor is here and would like to have a word with you."

"Yes, Mom," Gina said sheepishly as she followed her mom into the kitchen, where Mrs. O'Connor was seated at the table.

"Hello, Gina. How are you?"

"I'm fine, Mrs. O'Connor. How are you?"

Gina's mom motioned her daughter to take a seat. "Mrs. O'Connor came home from visiting Mr. O'Connor and found my garden stones all over her yard as if someone threw them and tried to hit Smokey with them. She found sticks too. Do you know anything about this?"

"No, Mom. I don't. I'm sorry, Mrs. O'Connor."

"That's fine, child. Do you know if the boy Jimmy, who lives across the street, had anything to do with it?"

Gina remembered what Jimmy said about being a tattletale. "No, I don't."

Gina's mom questioned how someone got into her backyard.

Gina shrugged. "I don't know," she said, her stomach twisting for lying to her mom and neighbor. Her mother excused her from the table. Gina stood, thinking about what she had done. She wanted to tell the truth, but she knew she'd never have anyone to play with again if she did. Jimmy would make sure of it.

As Gina walked away, she heard Mrs. O'Connor say she was going over to speak to Jimmy.

Gina was sure Jimmy would lie too.

It wasn't long before Gina learned Jimmy did lie. But, instead of saying he wasn't in the backyard, he said he was and that Gina had thrown the sticks and stones.

Mrs. O'Connor was again in the kitchen, and Gina sat at the table, this time being questioned about why she lied and why she threw the sticks and stones.

"Why would you do that?" her mother asked. "I am so disappointed that you would do such a thing and more disappointed that you would lie about it. That poor boy Jimmy said he tried many times to stop you. What's gotten into you?"

Tears streamed down Gina's face. "I'm sorry, Mom. I didn't mean to lie."

"Sorry isn't good enough. I want you to go next door, pick up every stone, bring it back where you found it, and pile the sticks to the curb. Your father will take care of them. And Gina, you'll carry the stones in your hands. No bag or bucket. That will give you plenty of time to think about what you did."

"Yes, Mom."

Gina went outside and picked up as many stones as she could fit in her hands, and she walked them to her backyard. Back and forth she went as Jimmy sat in his kitchen watching her through the window, laughing.

When Gina was finished, she went straight to her bedroom and cried herself to sleep.

The following day, Gina's mom woke her early.

"Get dressed and come have breakfast. You can walk with me to the store and help me carry the groceries home."

"Okay, Mom. I'll be down in a minute."

Gina sat quietly and ate her cereal. When she finished, she went to the bathroom to brush her teeth, and out the door she went with her mom.

They walked down the street and rounded the corner. Mrs. Anderson was sitting on her porch and greeted them.

"Mrs. Hawkins, you should be so proud of Gina. What she did yesterday was so noble."

Gina's mom was confused. "I'm sorry, but I don't know what you're talking about."

"Oh, I thought you knew. I had the baby outside in the playpen, and you know how our backyards join, well, Gina and the boy from across the street… I think Jimmy is his name… were in your backyard, and Jimmy threw stones at Mrs. O'Connor's dog. Gina pleaded with him many times to stop, but he didn't. I think your daughter was crying."

Gina's mom looked down at her daughter. "Is this true?"

Gina nodded.

Mrs. Anderson looked at Gina. "I wish there was something I could have done, but I couldn't leave the baby. So as soon as Mrs. O'Connor arrived home, I called her to let her know what Jimmy had done."

"Thank you for this," Gina's mom said. "I guess Mrs. O'Connor knew who did it before coming to my house."

"I did let her know it was the boy across the street," Mrs. Anderson said.

Gina's mom thanked Mrs. Anderson, and she tugged Gina's hand to start walking.

"You have a lot of explaining to do. First, you lied to Mrs. O'Connor; she must have known you lied. Can you tell me why you lied?"

Gina told her mother the truth—how she tried to stop Jimmy, what he told her would happen if she tattled, and how no one would ever play with her again.

"Let this be a lesson to you, Gina. You will always get caught in a lie, so tell the truth no matter how hard it may seem. You lied to protect Jimmy, and he lied so he wouldn't be in trouble. When we return from the store and put the groceries away, we need to walk across the street and speak with Jimmy's mother."

"Okay," Gina said shyly. "But will I be a tattletale?"

"No, you aren't a tattletale. But you need to apologize to Mrs. O'Connor for lying to her, and I think Jimmy needs to apologize to you both. I hope this has taught you that honesty is always the best policy."

CROSS MY HEART

Lively Benson was most at home at a dance studio. The jazz classes at a local dance studio were the highlight of each week, and she was always sad when the season ended. Sensing her passion and dedication, her parents converted their basement into a home studio with mirrored walls and floor mats to allow her to continue dancing all year. And dance she did! Lively spent all her free time in that studio. She felt safe there.

Like most new parents, when Lively was born, her mom and dad counted her fingers and toes. Ten little toes. Five little fingers on the right hand. But her left hand was different. Lively was born with a birth defect that affected her left hand. She was missing three fingers, and the two present were shorter than average. The condition had a long, tongue-twisting name that was difficult to pronounce, so Lively never tried.

Lively did not let her hand stop her from doing anything. Not only did she dance, but she played basketball and ran track at her middle school. When kids would ask her what was wrong with her hand, she would reply nothing was wrong. She was born how she was meant to be. Most kids her age were understanding when she explained. They would shrug their shoulders and say, "Okay. Whatever," before moving to the next topic.

But there was one person who would not move on: Ava Brown. The best dancer in the studio, she was also the prettiest and the most popular. The dance instructors fawned over her. Lively was able to avoid Ava at the studio during the season because they were in different classes. However, the off-season was a different story. Their parents were friends and liked to barbecue and have pool parties together. They took turns hosting and were together nearly every weekend.

School was out for the summer, and the end-of-the-season recital had wrapped up a week ago. Lively was missing the studio already.

"Mom, could we look for a dance class that I could take over the summer?" she asked as she watched her mother fold pool towels fresh from the dryer.

"Honey, you know that your father and I would if we could, but it just isn't in the cards with work and the cost." Her mother ran her fingers through Lively's thick brown hair.

Lively shooed her away. "You're going to mess up my hair." Lively had recently taken to styling her hair and wearing mascara.

"If it helps, your father can repaint your studio and freshen the mats. We have the budget for that."

Lively rolled her eyes and sighed. It was not the answer she was looking for. It was not a bad idea; the light pink paint looked babyish.

"Where is Dad? I want to ask him when he can start." Lively jumped from one foot to the next, raising her arms slowly from her sides up above her head while wiggling her fingers.

Her mother laughed. "You never stop dancing, do you?"

"Nope." Lively spun around on her toes, making a dramatic leap out of the laundry room toward the kitchen.

"Your father is outside cleaning the grill. The Browns are coming over for barbecue ribs. I've made a ton of food, so please don't ruin your supper with snacks."

Lively's excitement faded quickly when she realized that having Mr. and Mrs. Brown over for supper meant that Ava would also be coming.

"You can bring Ava down to your studio. Brainstorm ideas for paint colors," her mom said hesitantly. Her mom knew that Lively and Ava did not get along.

"You two could be good for each other. I wish you both would try." Lively followed her mother to the patio, simmering at the thought of bringing Ava into her studio.

"She makes fun of me, Mom. She makes fun of my hand. I don't want to be made fun of."

"I am sorry she makes fun of you. That's not nice. But I want you to try to put yourself in her shoes."

"What does that mean? You want me to try her shoes on?" Lively was confused.

"No, silly girl. I want you to imagine how you would feel if you were in her situation."

Lively was even more confused. What situation? Ava was the best dancer, and she was the most popular. She had all the best clothes and shoes. Being in her shoes seemed like it would make Lively happy. It did not explain why Ava made fun of her.

"Lively, all I want you to do is talk to her for a bit. Show her your studio and talk about dance. Listen to her. That is all I ask. Can you do that for me?"

"I'm hungry. A snack would help me think it over," Lively negotiated.

"One snack. That is it." Her mother ran her fingers through Lively's hair again.

"Mom!" Lively ducked away back into the kitchen. She grabbed a granola bar and retreated to the front porch.

Lively sat down in the big brown rocking chair. Her dad said this was a good thinking chair. Pointing her toes until her feet were fully extended, she barely tapped the surface of the porch. The rocker gently motioned backward and forward.

Lively thought about how she could approach Ava.

"Hey, Ava!"

"What's up, Ava?"

"Fine weather we have today, isn't it?"

Lively rehearsed aloud, but nothing felt right. What did her mother mean that not everything is what it seems on the outside? Why do parents have to be so cryptic? The thinking chair was not helping.

Before Lively could decide her approach, a sparkling black Range Rover pulled up in front of her house. Lively's stomach dropped. The Browns had arrived.

Mr. Brown held the door while Ava exited the vehicle like an actor stepping onto the red carpet.

"Hi, Lively!" The Browns were exuberant people, always beaming with happiness.

"Your mom tells me that you and Ava will be spending time in your studio. I am so happy. You girls can learn a lot from each other," Mrs. Brown said. She kissed Ava on top of the head, and

Mr. and Mrs. Brown skip-walked up the sidewalk and into the house.

Lively looked at Ava, who was frowning. Unlike her parents, Ava always looked sad, angry, or bored.

Ava looked at her nails, which she had bitten down to the nubs of her fingers.

"My parents have been talking all week about how much we can learn from each other. I have no idea what they are talking about." Ava rolled her eyes. "I swear they are speaking in code."

A nervous laugh escaped Lively. "I feel the same way. My mom has been talking like that all day. I'm so confused." Lively rubbed her left hand with her right hand. Lively hated that she had a nervous tic that drew attention to the one part about herself that she did not want people to notice.

"I don't know what I could learn from you. I am not like you at all. I have two whole hands." Ava stomped by Lively, waving her hands in front of Lively's face. Lively followed behind her. She was feeling angry now.

"Ava, you are not nice to me, and I will not listen to it. I am *not* going to bring you into my studio. You don't deserve to be there!" Lively was yelling now, tears forming in her eyes.

Ava stopped on the balls of her feet and slowly turned around. Lively could not believe what she was seeing. There were tears in Ava's eyes also. Instead of feeling bad for Ava, Lively felt even more angry.

"What do you have to cry about, little Miss Perfect? You have two whole hands. Awesome clothes. Your parents are rich and have a fancy truck. The dance instructors think you're the greatest dancer ever!" Lively was shaking, and the tears were streaming down her face.

Ava was crying now. "They only talk to me because of who my parents are. They don't care about me. My mom was a ballet dancer and a real stage ballerina. Our dance instructors want my mom to teach at the studio. And my dad, well, you are right. He is rich. The studio owner is always asking him for donations."

Lively could not believe what came out of her mouth next.

"I am sorry they treat you that way. That isn't nice at all."

Ava's mouth dropped open slightly. "What?"

"I am sorry. I would feel so, so… mad. And sad. I think." Lively had only thought of how good she would feel if the instructors showed her the kind of attention they gave Ava. Now that she knew the attention was fake and for all the wrong reasons, Lively could imagine Ava's anger and sadness when she was in the studio.

Ava wiped her face with the backs of her hands. "I just want them to leave me alone. Let me dance. That's how they treat you. I am jealous of you because of that."

"Wow." Lively could not think of anything better to say.

The two girls stood silently, Lively rubbing her left hand and Ava biting her nails and sniffling.

Ava broke the silence. "I'm sorry I said that about having two hands. That was so mean." Ava's face turned red, and the tears started to flow again.

"If you promise you won't say stuff like that anymore, I promise you can come into my studio whenever you want." Again, Lively could not believe what was coming out of her mouth.

"I promise. Cross my heart." Ava crossed her fingers over her heart and extended her hand to Lively. "Friends?"

Lively crossed her fingers over her heart and took Ava's hand with a big smile. "Friends."

SPREAD YOUR WINGS

Lauren Oliver loved books. She loved the smell of the cover and the feel of the paper. But, more than that, she loved the words on the pages. Her favorite word was hippopotamus. She thought it was fun to say and spell.

Lauren spent a lot of time reading. She was shy and didn't have many friends. Books were her friends.

At school, she often sat alone at lunch. She wanted to sit with others but was too shy to start a conversation. She had one friend, Darlene, whom she met at the ice skating rink last year, but Darlene went to a different school. At least they got to talk on the phone, and sometimes, they would go to each other's houses on the weekends.

Lauren was nervous because her teacher, Mr. Rose, gave her a sealed envelope to take home to her mother. She had no idea what it could be about. Her grades were good; in fact, they were excellent. She never got in trouble, was polite, and always used her manners.

When the school day ended, Lauren ran home as fast as she could. She wanted to know what was inside the mysterious envelope.

"Lauren, you've qualified for the school's spelling bee. The winner will go on to the state finals," her mother said, holding the letter for Lauren to see. "This is such an honor. I'm so proud of you."

Lauren looked at the letter, then at her mom.

"Mom, you know I can't do it. I can't get up in front of a lot of people. I wouldn't be able to even think of how to spell the word spell!"

"Nonsense, child. You can do it. This is an honor to be chosen. Don't let your shyness stop you from something so wonderful."

"I can't do it, Mom. I'm so sorry."

Lauren ran to her room, tears streaming from her eyes. She knew she was disappointing her mother, and she knew when her dad got home and learned she didn't want to be in the spelling bee, he'd be disappointed, too. After all, he'd told Lauren many times how he won the state spelling bee championship in sixth grade. Lauren was in fourth grade, but she knew words that many of her classmates didn't.

Lauren dried her eyes and telephoned Darlene.

"Do it!" Darlene shouted with excitement. "You need to do this, Lauren. It's an honor to be selected."

Lauren sighed. "That's what my mom said. I'm sure half of the school was picked. It's no big deal."

"You spell better than anybody I know. You can win. I know you can."

Darlene's excitement and encouragement didn't change Lauren's mind. She knew she'd freeze on a stage with the audience staring and judges watching her every move.

No, it was something she couldn't do.

Lauren went to school the following day prepared to tell Mr. Rose that she wasn't interested in participating in the spelling bee but appreciated the offer. Before she could say anything, Mr. Rose told her she'd be practicing after school with Jenny White.

"I called your mother to let her know you'll be in the school library after school for the next two weeks. She'll be picking you up. You'll leave at the side door by the gym as the main doors will be locked," Mr. Rose said.

Jenny White, Lauren thought. She was just as shy as Lauren. How could two shy girls practice together?

"Hey there, Lauren. It's great to see you," Jenny greeted as she sat across from Lauren. "I'm happy I was chosen to practice with you?"

Lauren froze, staring at Jenny. This wasn't the same Jenny she knew. Even though she hadn't seen Jenny this school year because they weren't in the same class, she remembered how quiet and shy she was just last year.

"Lauren, are you okay?" Jenny asked.

"I I, well, yes," Lauren answered quietly. "We should get started."

Jenny and Lauren went back and forth, spelling the words on Mr. Rose's list.

Lauren said the first word, and Jenny spelled it out. They took turns until they got to the last word. They did this every school day until the day of the spelling bee. But each day, Lauren and Jenny talked more and more. They talked about their favorite television shows and books and how much they love to ice skate.

"Can you go skating on Saturday afternoon? My mom can bring us and pick us up?" Jenny asked Lauren.

"I'll ask my mom. I'm sure she'll say yes."

"Great, here's my number. Call me tonight after you ask," Jenny said, handing Lauren a paper with her number.

When Lauren got home, she ran to the kitchen to ask her mom about skating with Jenny.

"Of course, you can go. I'll just need to speak to Jenny's mom before you go," Lauren's mom said, surprised by the request. "Lauren, I'm a little confused. How did this come about?"

"Jenny asked me," she said. "We both love to skate."

Lauren's mom smiled. Could it be her daughter was getting over her shyness?

Lauren couldn't wait for Saturday. She and Jenny planned to meet Darlene at the ice rink. When Jenny's mom arrived, Lauren was already outside waiting.

The three girls spent the afternoon skating, laughing, and trying not to fall. When the session ended, they got hot chocolate and sat at a table, waiting for Jenny's mom to pick them up.

"I'm so happy for you," Darlene said to Lauren. "How did you do it?"

"Do what?" Lauren asked.

"Make a new friend, and stop being so shy," Darlene answered.

"It just happened. We practiced together for the spelling bee and just started talking about other things."

"See how easy it is?" Jenny said. "That's how I did it. You just have to let it happen. Start a conversation with someone, and you'll see how you have things in common."

"I never thought I could talk to anyone," Lauren said.

"But you did," Jenny said excitedly. "And now you have a new friend, and I have two." She looked at Darlene. "I'm so happy you came today."

The trio vowed to spend more time together, and Lauren and Jenny rode to the spelling bee with Jenny's mom, picking up Darlene along the way to the school. Lauren's mom and dad rode with Jenny's dad. Not only did the girls become friends, but so did their parents.

Lauren's stomach felt like a big knot when they arrived, and her palms were sweaty. She was nervous but not scared to talk with other contestants while waiting her turn.

Finally, her name was called. She walked to the microphone and looked out to the audience. Her mom and dad were smiling, and so were Jenny's parents. Darlene gave her a thumbs-up as the judge announced the word Lauren was to spell: hippopotamus.

This was going to be a piece of cake.

NOTHING CAN STOP ME NOW

Every school day at recess, Eliza watched from her wheelchair as her classmates played on the playground. They would swing or teeter-totter, and others would round up enough players for a kickball game.

Eliza wanted nothing more than to join them. She tried to run and play like her classmates. Although she knew that she would never run, she wanted to play. She didn't understand why she couldn't swing or teeter-totter, but she knew she couldn't get out of her wheelchair without help, and her teacher didn't have the support needed to assist Eliza.

"Do you want to be in the sun or shade today?" her teacher, Mrs. Stone, would ask every day.

"The sun is fine," Eliza would answer each time. She didn't like being in the shade. She liked to feel the warmth on her skin. It was the only highlight of recess.

In the classroom, Eliza could do almost everything her classmates did. Because her wheelchair was larger than the desk chairs, she sat at a special table made to accommodate a wheelchair.

Eliza couldn't play gym like the others, but Mrs. Finch, the gym teacher, included Eliza as often as possible. Eliza could play catch and some of the other games. Mrs. Finch picked activities that Eliza could participate in as often as possible.

Sometimes, it just wasn't possible, and Eliza sat on the sidelines watching.

Eliza had a lot of friends, but none knew how sad she felt because she couldn't play at recess. She didn't want to tell anyone, not even her best friend Casey. Eliza didn't want anyone to feel sorry for her. She liked that the rest of her classmates treated her like everyone else and didn't want anyone to feel sorry for her.

Sometimes, Casey would ask her questions about not being able to run like the others, and Eliza always answered that it didn't bother her. She did like it when winter came, and recess was held inside, usually playing board games or reading. Eliza's favorite indoor recess was when the girls would sit together and talk. She thought it was nice they could do that. Some kids, like Jason Peterson, would fall asleep in the beanbag chair and snore. The girls would giggle and talk about ways to wake him, but they knew they wouldn't try. It was fun coming up with ways, though.

Every day at lunchtime, Eliza's classmates took turns wheeling her to the cafeteria. Her wheelchair was electric, and she could get herself there, but her classmates enjoyed pushing her there and back.

Sometimes, one of her classmates would ask Eliza why she couldn't walk. She would explain the car accident she was in and how she remembers running and playing with other kids.

"I have walked before, and I could run," she'd say when asked. "But after the accident, I couldn't move my legs like I used to. I can still move them a little, but it's okay because I am happy my mom, dad, and brother didn't get hurt. I would be sad if they were."

Eliza vowed never to let her sadness show. As much as she tried to hide it, Casey saw it. She saw it every time Eliza watched the class play at recess, which bothered her.

"I'll sit with you," Casey offered every day, and every day, Eliza refused.

"I'm fine. Play with the others. I like watching when you play kickball and get out," Eliza said with a laugh. "You crack me up."

"Ha, ha," Casey said as she ran off. "Nobody will get me out today!"

Suddenly, Eliza wasn't coming to school. She was absent for an entire week, then another and another. Casey would call Eliza's house, but no one ever answered. Mrs. Stone would know, but she only announced to the class that Eliza would not be attending for a long time.

Two months passed, and Eliza was still not in school. Casey and the others figured she and her family must have moved away, and Eliza left without saying goodbye.

Then, three months later, the class went outside for recess on a warm, sunny day. They were playing kickball when someone called out to them.

"Hey, do you need a pinch-kicker?"

The game stopped as everyone turned to see who it was.

"Eliza!" a chorus rang out. "Is that really you, Eliza?"

The classmates ran over to her.

"What?"

"How?"

"For real?"

A flood of questions came pouring out of their mouths.

Eliza flashed a broad smile.

"I went to a hospital in Boston and had two surgeries to repair my legs," she explained. "I only need these crutches now; soon, I might not need them. I am having a lot of therapy and can kick a ball. I can't run yet, but I am doing my best to get so I can."

Eliza told her classmates that not everyone can have surgeries to help them walk again, but her injury was eligible for the surgery and worth trying. Fortunately, it worked for her.

"It doesn't work for everyone, but technology is making a lot of advances, so people can do more if they are in a wheelchair. So, let's get this game going again!"

As everyone cheered, Casey helped Eliza walk to the kickball field.

"You can kick for me," she said as they reached the field. "I am up now, so let's see what you can do."

With Casey's help, Eliza stepped to the plate. Bobby Bonnell pitched the ball, and Eliza kicked a grounder to third base. Casey ran and made it to first base.

"Great kick," Casey yelled.

"Nothing can stop me now!" Eliza answered as she prepared to kick for Sarah DuBois. "Nothing at all!"

THE BIG SURPRISE

Eva hurried to school Monday morning to try out for the school play. The tryouts were held before classes started, so Eva needed to wake up earlier than usual. She didn't mind. She wanted nothing more than to win a part in "The Wizard of Oz."

She walked into the auditorium and looked around until she found her friend Paloma.

"I'll never get a part," Eva said. "Look how many are here."

Paloma agreed. "How will we all get to try out before classes start?"

"I don't know, but we'll soon find out," Eva said.

Mr. Zollo entered the stage and walked to the podium. He tapped the microphone a few times to make sure it was on.

"Ladies and gentlemen, we have a great crowd here today, which pleases me," Mr. Zollo announced. "Because there are more than expected, you'll be trying out in pairs. Be prepared to come to the stage quickly when I call your name. I assume you've all practiced the lines I handed out last week. As you'll be in pairs, feel free to ad-lib if you don't want to read the same lines as your partner."

Eva turned to Paloma and whispered, "I hope we go last to see how the others do."

"Me too. We're supposed to sit in the cafeteria when we're done, and that's so boring."

Their hope of being last was shattered when Mr. Zollo called them to be first.

"Eva and Paloma, please come to the stage. As you both have been in plays before, you can show the others how a tryout should go. We have many new faces here today."

Eva read the prepared lines, and Paloma ad-libbed. When they finished, Mr. Zollo announced that they gave a remarkable performance, and that's how a tryout should be done.

"Don't simply read the lines; show movement and facial expressions. Thank you, Eva and Paloma. You can go to the cafeteria now."

Paloma looped her arm through Eva's. "Maybe we'll get a part. He did use us as an example," she said.

"I sure hope so. It would make sitting in the cafeteria for thirty minutes worthwhile." Eva laughed. "We should find out tomorrow if we got a part."

"I know you will. I'm not so sure about if I will."

"Oh, Paloma. You'll get a part. You're so good!"

The wait to learn who got a part didn't take long. Eva and Paloma were called to the auditorium after school.

"Everyone, when I call you, please come to the stage to pick up the script. Your lines are highlighted in yellow. Please study them and be prepared to begin practice after school each day for the next three weeks. Make sure your parents know you'll be staying, and a late bus will be provided," Mr. Zollo said. "You can ride the late bus even if you normally walk."

Eva took Paloma's hand as they waited. "Good luck," she whispered. "I'm so nervous.

"Paloma, please come to the stage."

Eva watched as Paloma approached Mr. Zollo.

"Will you accept the role of Dorothy?" Mr. Zollo asked Paloma.

She squealed, and everyone clapped. With a huge smile, Paloma walked off the stage with her script.

Mr. Zollo announced the wizard, scarecrow, lion, and Tin Man, then called Eva to the stage.

"Will you accept the role of the good witch?" he asked Eva.

"Yes, yes!" she said. "I would be honored."

With scripts in hand, Eva and Paloma walked home together. Eva couldn't wait to tell her mother and father. She was so happy to be playing the good witch. She was happy, too, that Paloma got the female lead.

Paloma was excited, but she was also sad. Her father couldn't attend the play because he was deployed overseas, serving his country in the Marines. He wasn't due home until the school year ended—too late for him to see the play. Still, she was happy that Mr. Zollo said he would try to arrange for Paloma's father to watch it on a video call, and it would be recorded so he could watch it later.

For the next three weeks, Eva and Paloma practiced, and as the big opening night was days away, Paloma grew sadder.

"My dad won't get to see me," she told Eva. "The yellow brick road is too far away."

Eva put her arm around Paloma. "I know it's not easy. I'd want my dad here too, and he will be for both of us."

"I know," Paloma said. "My dad is doing good things, and I know he'd be here if he could."

The big night came, and Mr. Zollo stood at the podium to address the audience.

"As we present to you our play, it is a reminder that when we follow the right road, we can meet the man behind the curtain. Tonight, you'll meet the man behind the curtain thanks to one student with a kind heart, a great idea, and the courage to seek help. Please welcome Dorothy and the good witch."

"What's he doing?" Paloma asked as they walked onto the stage from the room to the left.

Eva shrugged. "Who knows."

"Ladies and gentlemen, we have a little preview tonight for you. You all know how the play ends. The man behind the curtain is exposed. Tonight, we're going to do something different. Tonight, we're going to begin the play at the end," Mr. Zollo announced.

Sighs and gasps of confusion filled the auditorium.

"Dorothy, would you do the honor of pulling the curtain open."

"Sure, I guess," Paloma answered, confused by the strange request.

Paloma pulled the cord, and the curtain opened. She let out a scream and started crying. There stood her dad in full uniform, smiling with open arms. She ran to him and hugged him so hard he almost fell over.

"I can't believe this! How did you get here... I mean, how were you able?" Paloma asked through happy tears.

"Your friend Eva. Her dad works for the government in defense," her father said, hugging her again. "Now, I'm going to sit in the audience with your mother and watch my daughter give the performance of a lifetime."

Paloma's father gave his daughter one more hug before exiting the stage.

Paloma scanned the stage for Eva, and when she saw her off to the side, she walked over and hugged her.

"How did you get my dad here?" Paloma asked, still crying happy tears.

"We'll talk after the play," Eva said.

Mr. Zollo introduced the cast, and they received a standing ovation at the end.

"Before everyone leaves, I'd like to thank Eva Williamson for the compassion and kindness she showed her friend Paloma. Sergeant Major Gregory Marshall would like to come to the stage now."

Loud applause broke out as Paloma's father walked to the stage. He presented Eva with a dozen red roses.

"Thank you, Eva, for ensuring I arrived tonight and convincing your dad to get me a three-day pass. It means the world to me," he said.

The audience roared with applause as Paloma and her father walked off the stage.

"This has been the best day of my life," Paloma said.

Her father took her hand. "And there will be many, many more."

DON'T JUMP TO CONCLUSIONS

Gabrielle looked over at the empty seat in her math class.

"Again?" she said to Ace, who sat behind her. "Why is Danelle always absent? Do you think she moved to another school?"

"She must have," Ace said. "It's kind of weird that nobody's said anything. It's like she's disappeared."

"I hope she isn't sick," Gabrielle said as Miss Potter told her to turn around.

Gabrielle and Danelle had been good friends since first grade. Their teacher called them the "Double Elles," and they would giggle. By the time they reached fifth grade, the nicknames had stuck, and they were known as the "Double Elles" to almost everyone in the school.

Because Gabrielle and Danelle were such good friends, their classmates assumed Gabrielle knew why Danelle hadn't been in school. The more time that passed, the more Gabrielle was asked. Yet, she asked others, including Ace, who was also a good friend of Danelle's, had no idea why.

Danelle was at school one day and gone the next, and the next, and the next. Gabrielle was concerned because she hadn't heard from Danelle, not even a phone call or text message.

The days passed with the seat staying empty in math class. During lunch in the cafeteria, everyone started talking about the mysterious absence.

"My mother said she and her family left town," Sandy Blake said. "My mother knows someone whose cousin sold their house and said they moved a month ago."

"That's not true," Jose Padula said. "Danelle's mom shops at my dad's store all the time. She was just there the other day."

"Have your dad ask why Gabrielle hasn't been in school," MaryKate Andrews said. "That's easy enough."

"I'm not going to do that," Jose said. "It's not my business, and it's not anyone's business. If she wanted us to know why she's not here, don't you think she'd tell one of us?"

"Maybe she can't. Maybe she can't talk," MaryKate said. "I heard she can't talk."

"Who told you that?" Gabrielle asked MaryKate.

"I can't tell. It's a secret."

The next day, everyone talked about Danelle and how she could not speak. Some kids said she had an accident, and others said she was sick and couldn't talk.

Gabrielle didn't believe any of it. She didn't like the rumors that were spread about her friend.

"Ace, did you hear anything about Danelle?" she turned around and asked before math class started.

"I heard a few things about her being sick and being in a boating accident," Ace answered. "I don't think any of it's true. I think it's strange that she's not here, and we don't know why, but I'm sure we'll find out sooner or later."

Gabrielle couldn't concentrate on her math lesson. She wondered how Danelle was keeping up with schoolwork if she wasn't coming to school. Missing a lot of lessons would be hard to catch up because they've been learning a lot. Soon, it would be time for final exams and the end of the school year. Gabrielle hoped Danelle would be back before school ended. If not, she might never see her again, especially if it's true that she moved away.

More days passed, which meant more rumors about why Danelle wasn't in school. Sandy insisted Danelle and her family sold their house and moved out of town. MaryKate insisted Danelle was unable to speak and would never return to school.

Neither Ace nor Jose wanted any part of the rumors, nor did Gabrielle. She wanted to know why her friend wasn't coming to school and if she was okay.

"Is her mom still going to your dad's store?" she asked Jose.

"Yes, my dad said she was there yesterday," he said. "She hasn't moved. MaryKate is making that up."

"But why would she do that?" Ace asked.

"I think everybody just wants to know where Danelle is and why she isn't coming to school," Jose answered.

Gabrielle sighed. "She hasn't been here in five or six weeks, and she hasn't tried to get ahold of me."

"I'm sure the principal knows why she's not here," Ace said. "And probably the teachers."

"Yeah, everybody but us," Gabrielle said.

Later that day, Gabrielle was sitting at the dinner table with her family when her cell phone rang.

"Mother, may I see who it is?" she asked.

"You may be excused," her mother said as Gabrielle jumped from her seat and ran to the living room to get her phone.

"Mom, mom, it was Danelle. I missed her call."

"Well, call her back," Gabrielle's mother said, happy her daughter had finally heard from her friend.

Gabrielle rushed to her bedroom and called Danelle. She was thrilled when she heard her answer.

"Where are you? Where have you been? Why aren't you in school?" Gabrielle asked in rapid succession.

"Slow down, Elle," Danelle said and laughed. "I'll explain if you give me a chance."

"Tell me, tell me. I've been so worried."

Danelle explained how she had fallen in the bathtub and broken her leg in three places. She needed special surgery, so she had to go out of town to a bigger hospital where a surgeon knew how to fix her leg.

"I was in a big cast for six weeks, and my leg was elevated. When the cast came off, I had to have therapy to learn how to use it again. I couldn't call you, Gabrielle. I am so sorry. I didn't have my cell phone with me, and I didn't have a phone in my room. I wouldn't have been able to reach it, anyway," Danelle said.

"Oh, that sounds so painful. Are you okay now?" Gabrielle asked.

"It hurt, but the doctors made me all better, and I can walk now. I have a scar. I'll show it to you at school tomorrow."

"You're coming to school tomorrow?" Gabrielle was so excited. It was the best news she had all week.

"I'll be there, and I can't wait to see you and Ace."

"How did you keep up with schoolwork?" Gabrielle asked.

Danelle explained she had a tutor who came to the hospital three times a week and got all the work from her teachers every Friday.

"They emailed my tutor everything you were working on, and I did my work and emailed it."

Gabrielle couldn't wait to get to school the next morning. She skipped breakfast and hurried out the door. She hugged Danelle when she saw her, and they walked to math together.

Miss Potter welcomed Danelle back to school.

"Class, you've all missed Danelle, and so have I," Miss Potter said. "I also heard all the rumors going around the school, and I hope you all learn a lesson that you shouldn't jump to conclusions. Know the facts before you say anything about anybody or any situation."

MaryKate and Sandy apologized to Danelle at lunch for jumping to conclusions and spreading rumors.

"Jumping to conclusions isn't good," Danelle said. "And neither is jumping out of the bathtub to answer your cell phone."

MaryKate, Sandy, Ace, and Jose couldn't wait to hear the rest of the real story.

SYLVIA'S WISH

Sylvia was happy that she would spend two weeks of summer vacation at her Aunt Louise's. Her aunt lived in a small town three hours away from Sylvia's home. Not only did Sylvia like getting away from the big city where she lived, but her aunt's neighborhood had a lot of kids her age who looked forward to her visit each summer.

Sylvia was treated special by the neighborhood kids. They would gather every morning at her aunt's to play together.

And play they did, from early morning until it was time for supper. They would barely break for lunch and sometimes eat together at Aunt Louise's picnic table.

Sylvia had a lot of friends when she visited her aunt, a lot more than she did at home. She enjoyed every minute of her vacation, but it was hard to leave when the two weeks had passed.

"She's here, she's here," Kota, Beth, Dayton, Josie, Anton, and Roger shouted when Sylvia got out of her mother's car. The friends gathered around Sylvia as she hugged each one.

"I've got to unpack and talk to Aunt Louise. I'll come play later," Sylvia said.

She went inside and, after a lovely chat with her aunt, Sylvia went outside to be with her friends. They played all kinds of games until it was time to go home.

Aunt Louise smiled when Sylvia walked through the door. She was covered in dirt and grass stains, a sign of a fun time.

"Hop right in the tub, young lady, and I'll fix you a bedtime snack. Bring me your clothes so I can wash them."

Sylvia took her bath and got ready for bed. She went to the living room to say goodnight to her aunt.

"I had so much fun here, Aunt Louise," she said, sitting beside her on the couch. "I wish I could stay here forever. I wish I had this many friends back home."

"Do you try to make friends?" Aunt Louise asked.

"Not really. It's different in the city. The kids I go to school with live too far away to play. Can I live here forever?"

Aunt Lousie chuckled. "I don't think you'd like living here all the time. Josie and Anton are like you. They don't live here. They come to stay with their father for the summer. Kota and Beth live here, but I don't see them outside much once school starts, and Roger is homeschooled, so he's inside most days. Dayton plays sports, so he's very busy."

"But I don't have friends to play with when I go home. I have a few school friends, but we never get together after school."

"You don't have any friends at all close by?"

"No, Aunt Louise. That's why I love coming here every summer. Well, I love coming to see you, too!"

"We can talk more in the kitchen. I've made you popcorn," Aunt Louise said, waving her hand for Sylvia to join her.

"Are you sure I can't live here?" Sylvia pleaded.

"Sylvia, I would love to have you, but I'm afraid I could not take care of a ten-year-old, and your parents would miss you. And what about your dog Sallie?"

"Sallie could move here with me," Sylvia answered.

"I'm afraid I can't have a dog in the house. I sneeze when I'm around pets. That's why I don't have any."

Sylvia understood, kissed her aunt goodnight, and went to her room. She loved that Aunt Lousie kept it special just for her. It was painted in her favorite color—pink—and she had toys, games, and puzzles. Aunt Louise kept the room just for Sylvia. She promised no one else would sleep there.

The following day, the gang came to the door early, and Aunt Louise invited them in for pancakes and eggs. Sylvia poured them orange juice, saying, "I wish I could do this every day for the rest of my life."

"Me too," Kota said. "I wish you were here all the time."

The others agreed. Sylvia smiled. She was so happy to have so many friends but wished she never had to leave.

The days passed, and Sylvia enjoyed playing with her summer friends. They played games, swam in Roger's pool, and went to the playground a block away. Aunt Louise let them go without her, knowing the park was supervised.

One morning, Aunt Louise invited all the children in for breakfast. She told them she had an idea.

"When you go home for dinner, ask if you can come back, and we will go outside to catch fireflies and play some games in the dark. This is Sylvia's last night here, and I'd like to make it special," Aunt Louise said.

"It's my last night?" Sylvia asked. A tear rolled down her cheek. "Already?"

"I'm sorry, dear. Your mother and father are coming to get you tomorrow. They miss you."

"I miss them, too. But I'm going to miss my friends. I wish I could stay longer."

"I know, dear," Aunt Louise said. "Now, let's eat so you can get outside to play."

When breakfast was finished, the children helped Aunt Louise clear the table and then rushed outside to start a game of tag. Later, they would go swimming in Roger's pool. His mother invited all the kids to an afternoon of swimming and lemonade. Sylvia thought it was a wonderful way to spend her final day with her friends.

After dinner, everyone gathered at Aunt Louise's. She handed out jars and led them to her backyard to catch fireflies. They ran around and chased the bugs as their light blinked.

"This is so much fun," Josie said. "I wish I could do this every night."

"I do, too!" Beth said as she caught her first firefly.

"When we've finished, we are releasing the fireflies," Aunt Louise said. "That's why there are holes in the jar lids. The fireflies can breathe until we let them go."

"This is great!" Kota squealed. "The fireflies look so cool in the jar when they light up. This was the best idea ever!"

Aunt Louise told them to count their fireflies and release them. Kota was excited as he caught the most.

When everyone released their fireflies, they played a game of tag with flashlights that Aunt Louise brought out.

The children played until nine-thirty, and Aunt Louise walked each one home.

Sylvia hugged them goodbye and cried as she returned to the house with Aunt Louise.

"I wish I could stay another week, please, please," Sylvia begged.

"I'm sorry, dear. I know how much fun you have when you're here, and I love having you." Aunt Louise took Sylvia's hand. "It's such a beautiful night. Shall we take some ice cream from the freezer and enjoy it on the porch?"

"Sure," Sylvia said, her head hung low.

Aunt and niece ate ice cream, and Sylvia looked up to the sky and wished upon a star.

"Star light, star bright, please grant me my wish tonight."

"Sylvia, I know you wish you could stay, but sometimes, we can't always get what we wish for, and we need to be grateful for what we have."

"I know, Auntie, but I get bored at home. Here, I have friends. And I don't get to see them or talk to them until I return next summer," Sylvia pouted.

Aunt Louise perked up. "I have an idea. I will give you envelopes with stamps with all your friends' addresses, and I'll do the same for them with your address."

"Really? Do you think they will write to me?" Sylvia asked excitedly.

"I'm sure they will. I'll remind them if you don't hear from them, but it's an excellent way to keep in touch."

Sylvia kissed her aunt goodnight and went to her room. She tried to fall asleep, but all she could think about was leaving. Finally, she gave in and fell fast asleep.

When she woke the next morning, she was surprised to see her friends at the breakfast table.

"We're having an envelope exchange!" Beth said. "We're going to write you letters, and you better answer back!"

"I will," Sylvia said. She turned to Aunt Louise. "I am so grateful you did this for me, and I'm grateful even though I didn't get my wish. I got something just as good—keeping up with my friends all year."

AVERIE'S PERSEVERANCE

Averie did not want to go inside the school. She didn't know anyone, and her English wasn't very good. She missed her hometown of Montreal and her friends.

Averie had to move to the United States because her father accepted a job in New York City. He moved the family to a suburb and enrolled Averie in a nice elementary school a block from their new home. She wouldn't need to take a bus and could sleep later since school was so close. The bus came early in Montreal, and Averie had a long ride to school.

"You need to go inside," Averie's mother said, taking her hand and tugging at it. "Your teachers will help you learn English better than I have. You will learn to write it and not just speak it."

"But, Momma, I don't want to go to school here. Please take me back to Montreal," Averie said in French.

"I know you don't want to go to school, but you must. You will have a good day once you get inside."

Averie's mother kissed her on the cheek and turned to walk away. She heard Averie sniffle but knew she had to leave.

Averie sat at her desk and watched her classmates walk into the classroom before the final bell rang. Some looked at her, and some walked past her without looking or saying anything. This made Averie feel more uncomfortable than she had been feeling. She knew she'd never make friends, and with her broken

English, she was certain she'd never have friends at her new school.

The teacher, Mr. Cardinal, called the class to attention and introduced Averie.

"Averie comes to us from Montreal, Quebec, Canada. Can anyone tell me where Canada is located?"

Luca Jamerson raised his hand. "It's above the United States," he said proudly.

"Very good," Mr. Cardinal said. "How do you know this? We haven't studied it yet, but we will this year."

"My mom is from Montreal," Luca answered. "We go there a lot to see my grandparents."

"That's wonderful. Perhaps you can show Averie around the school."

"I'd be happy to," Luca said.

"Please go now," Mr. Cardinal said. "Averie, Luca will show you the gym, cafeteria, and art and music rooms. He'll show you the restrooms and the nurse's room."

Averie stood and followed behind Luca.

"Would you be more comfortable if I spoke to you in French?" Luca asked, noticing Averie's broken English.

"You speak French?" Averie asked, surprised.

"Yes, I do. Would you like me to help you with your English? I know it's not easy to learn. I can help you during lunch. We have about twenty minutes after we eat to sit and talk. I could help you then."

"That would be nice," Averie said. She was thrilled to meet a new friend, and she wanted help with her English so she wouldn't feel out of place.

Averie and Luca walked the halls and showed Averie all the places she would need to know. They walked slowly and talked the entire time. Averie felt comfortable with Luca. He understood what it was like being in a new school and not fluent in the language.

Averie was already feeling better when she returned to the classroom. Mr. Cardinal was patient and helped her when she didn't understand something. Reading was hard for Averie because she learned to speak English but didn't spend a lot of time working on sight words and spelling.

When the lunch bell rang, Luca walked Averie to the cafeteria. He sat with her, and they conversed in French and some English. Averie was so happy to have someone who could speak her native tongue. Luca was fluent in French and English and knew little Spanish. Averie was impressed with his language skills.

"You are smart," Averie told Luca. "How did you get so smart?"

"I read a lot," he answered. "I like to read, and I don't have many friends, so I don't go to many places. How about you?"

"I have no friends here," Averie said. "I have some back home. Well, what was my home."

"Would you like to be my friend?" Luca asked. "I can help you learn English after school sometimes."

"Yes, I will be your friend," Averie said. "I'm not sure I'll ever learn English the way you know it."

"Sure, you will. It just takes time."

Averie and Luca started meeting at Averie's house after school every day. They would study English together and have a snack when they were finished. Luca's mother would pick him up promptly at four-thirty.

The days passed, and Averie thought she wasn't progressing with reading. She was doing better with speaking, and Luca was proud of how much better she was doing. Even Mr. Cardinal commended her for her hard work in learning a new language.

Still, she struggled with reading and writing. Averie was frustrated. She wanted to give up. She wasn't making a lot of progress, and whenever she tried to cancel the after-school study sessions, Luca wouldn't let her. Even Averie's mother wasn't letting her cancel.

"I just don't want to do this anymore," Averie cried to her mother as she was tucked into bed. Averie thought she was too old to be tucked in, but her mother insisted and would sing her a song or read her a short story in English.

"Averie, honey, we will be living here for a long time. You need to learn English so you can do well in school."

"I will move back to Montreal when I'm old enough, so I don't need to know English that well. Besides, all this time learning English will make me forget French."

"You will never forget French," her mother said. "You never forget your native language, even if you don't speak it in a long time. It's always there for you."

Averie said goodnight and asked her mother to turn out her light.

"Tomorrow will be a new day," her mother said as she left Averie's room. "Each day will bring you closer to your goal of reading and writing in English."

The next day at school, Luca didn't sit with Averie at lunch or talk to her all day. Averie didn't know why, and she wasn't too worried. She thought maybe Luca was just having a bad day. But she knew something was wrong when he didn't show up at her house for their study session.

"Why don't you call him?" Averie's mother said. "Don't be afraid to ask him what's going on."

Averie shook her head and went to her room. She wasn't going to call Luca. He could call or say something at school if she wanted to talk to her.

Three days passed with Luca not talking to Averie in school or showing up for their study session. Averie sat alone in the cafeteria and watched Luca talking and laughing with other kids. She never saw him talking to many other kids, so she was happy he found new friends but sad he was no longer hers.

After school, Averie decided to ask Luca what was going on. She waited for him to come out of the school.

"Luca, why are you mad at me?" she asked. "Did I do something wrong?"

"Averie, I've been working with you for a month, and you don't seem interested in learning to read and write in English. You're just wasting my time."

Averie started to cry. "I-I just want to live in Montreal. And the English is hard."

"Listen, Averie. Learning anything new takes perseverance. You don't have that. I'm not trying to be mean. I'm being honest."

"Per…ser… what?" she asked.

"Perseverance. It means not giving up. It means doing something even if it's hard," Luca explained.

"Perseverance," Averie said slowly. "If you come to study with me tomorrow, I will show you perseverance."

"I'll think about it," Luca said.

Averie walked home from school, saddened that she discouraged Luca and made him feel unappreciated. She walked into her house and saw Luca sitting in the living room with her mother.

"What are you doing here?" Averie asked.

Luca stood and smiled. "Well, I decided if you can have perseverance, so can I. Let's get started on today's lesson!"

PRACTICE MAKES PERFECT

Elena wanted nothing more than to make her school's cheerleading squad. She practiced every day in front of her bedroom mirror, making sure each move was just right.

Her mother bought her pom-poms so she could practice using them. Elena moved her bed and rearranged her dressers and desk, so she had room to jump. She went to her backyard to do cartwheels. She didn't forget anything. She even watched videos on the internet of cheerleading squads at competitions.

Elena knew she might not make the team. It was going to be very competitive. Many girls signed up for tryouts. When she left school Friday, thirty names were on the list, and there was still a week left to sign up. That also meant one more week to practice.

Elena's best friend Susan didn't want Elena to try out.

"You won't make it because you aren't popular. Only the popular girls make it whether they're good or not," Susan said.

"I don't care. I want to try out, and if I don't make it, I'll be okay," Elena said.

"You'll be sorry and feel bad," Susan said. "You probably won't make the first cut because they want to make sure the popular girls make it."

Elena didn't understand why her best friend would discourage her from doing something she desperately wanted. She worked hard for weeks to perfect her moves. She convinced her mother to let her take gymnastics so she could learn to do the splits and cartwheels.

For a year, Elena went to gymnastics class every Saturday morning for an hour. She enjoyed it, and even if she didn't make the cheerleading squad this year, she would try again next year and the next and the next until she made it.

Elena knew Susan wasn't wholly wrong. It did seem like the popular girls were cheerleaders, and that's why she practiced so much. Practice makes perfect, her mother would tell her.

When Elena didn't understand long division, her teacher told her the more she practiced, the easier it would become. Her teacher was right. Elena practiced long division every day for two weeks, and it became easy. It was so easy she'd forgotten how she didn't understand it.

Cheerleading was the same. Elena learned by watching videos, going to her school's basketball game, and watching the cheerleaders. Sometimes, she didn't pay attention to the game at all. Her mother told her she should because it's essential to understand the game and when to cheer.

Elena started watching basketball games on television, and her brother Ben explained what was happening. Ben was a year younger, but he was a big help to Elena and knew how much she wanted to be a cheerleader. He was always ready to go outside to spot his sister when she did cartwheels.

"You got this," Ben would tell her with every perfect cartwheel. "You will make the squad. You are so good!"

Elena could only hope Ben was right. She thought about what Susan said but didn't let it bother her.

"Hey, El, I see you signed up to try out for cheerleading," Nancy said as she sat next to Elena in music class. "I don't know why you're doing it. I know I'll make it, and my friends will too."

Nancy was one of the most popular girls in middle school. She had a lot of friends, and she was on the cheer squad last year, so Elena was sure she'd be on it again. There were seven openings, and the list of girls trying out was growing.

Elena checked the list each day before leaving school. It was thirty-eight the day before tryouts, and she hoped no one else signed up. Thirty-eight are trying out for seven positions. Elena knew the odds weren't good, especially since Susan and Maria would likely make it because they were on the team last year. And Susan will probably make sure her friends make it.

Coach Sari Ford saw Elena reading the list.

"Hi, Elena. I'm Coach Sari Ford, but you can call me Coach Sari. I see you'll be trying out tomorrow. Have you ever done cheerleading?"

"It's nice to meet you, Coach Sari. I've never been on a cheer squad but have been practicing. I want to make it. It's all I've ever wanted to do."

Coach Sari smiled. "It takes a lot of practice. I wish there were more openings, but the school only allows me to have fourteen on the squad. I choose two alternates who practice with us and fill in when one of the girls is absent."

"I would be happy being an alternate if I'm not good enough yet," Elena said. "I know with so many trying out, I don't have a good chance."

"That's not the attitude to have," Coach Sari said. "Think positively; if you've practiced, you should do well."

Elena could barely sleep that night. She was so excited. She couldn't wait for tryouts.

Ben waited by the door for his sister so they could walk to school together. Along the way, he gave her a pep talk.

"Remember, sis, you can do this. Just don't get all nervous and jittery. Stay calm and remember what you've been practicing."

"I will, Ben. I'm not nervous. I'm more excited than anything. I can't wait for the school day to end. It's going to feel like forever waiting for tryouts to start."

Susan sat with Elena at lunch and tried to talk Elena out of trying out.

"Why are you doing this?" Elena asked. "Why don't you want me to try out?"

"I just don't want you to be disappointed," Susan answered. "Cheerleading is for the popular girls. You should try out for track. You run fast, and almost everyone makes the team."

"Well, you have no confidence in me," Elena said. "You're supposed to be my friend and give me encouragement."

Susan pushed her broccoli around with her fork. "I can't stand broccoli. Why do they give it to us?"

Elena sighed. "You're changing the subject, but that's okay. I guess you aren't a true friend. I don't like broccoli either, but it has nothing to do with your lack of confidence in me."

"Sorry," Susan said. She picked up her tray, stood, and walked away.

Elena didn't understand why her friend acted that way but didn't have time to worry about it.

The bell rang, signaling the end of the school day. Elena walked as fast as she could to the gym. When she arrived, she was surprised to see Susan.

"Why are you here?" Elena asked her friend.

"Why do you think? I'm trying out."

"But your name isn't on the list."

"Look again," Susan said, pointing. "I talked to the coach, and she said it was okay for me to try out."

Just then, Coach Sari called to the girls to line up.

"We're going to start with voices. I'll go down the line, and you need to shout, 'Go, team, go. Win tonight,' when I point to you. At the end, I will call the names of those who made this cut."

As Coach went down the line, everyone shouted and made the cut. Next, they had to do a short cheer with their pom-poms. Three girls were eliminated, two never showed, and one girl had scratched her name off the list, so thirty-three girls were left.

The coach had them perform drill after drill, dropping the number even more as some were eliminated.

With only twenty girls left, it was time to do cartwheels, high jumps, and splits.

Elena was confident she did well. She left feeling good because she did her best. The coach said she would post the names of those who made it the following day by noon. That gave Elena plenty of time to check before she went to the cafeteria for lunch.

She didn't need to wait for lunch. Nancy sat next to her in music class.

"Congratulations, I see you made the team."

"How do you know?" Elena asked.

"The list is posted. I just saw it on the way here. You made it. I didn't," she said.

"Wait, what do you mean you didn't make it?" Elena was surprised.

"I guess I was too confident. I thought if I were in the squad last year, I'd be on it automatically this year, but that's not how it works, and I didn't practice at all," Nancy said, tears forming in her eyes.

"I don't know what to say," Elena said. "I'm so sorry."

"Your friend Susan made the team too. You're a lucky girl," Nancy said.

Later, when Elena said Susan, she congratulated her.

"I'm happy for you, but I don't understand why you didn't want me to try out," Elena said.

"You practiced so much every day. I was afraid I wouldn't make it if I had to compete against you," Susan said. "I'm sorry. It was wrong of me. I practiced every day, too, and I didn't tell you."

"It's okay," Elena said. "We both made it. That's all that matters."

Susan hugged her friend. "I guess for both of us, practice made perfect."

A LISTENING EAR

Ring! Ring! Ring!

"Ugh!" came a loud groan. Slowly, the mound of blankets moved, and a thin, pale arm slithered from underneath. Contrary to its frail appearance, the arm slammed the alarm into complete silence.

Peace had been achieved.

It wasn't ten minutes later when Stacy toppled the blankets she had been buried under—an expression of utter horror hijacking her face.

"I'm late!" she screamed.

Granted, sleeping in could be listed as Stacy's most loved hobby; she hated it right now. In an extreme panic, Stacy pulled clothes from her wardrobe, not caring if they paired well.

She got ready in record time and flew to the kitchen. Yet, instead of the aroma of freshly baked pancakes, what greeted her was the fragrance of dish soap. The kitchen held none of its usual warmth because the person who gave life to it was missing. Stacie found a note from her mother on the kitchen counter, next to a Pop-Tart.

Honey,

I had to go to work early this morning. I'm sorry for not meeting you for breakfast, but I promise to make it up to you later.

Love,

Mom

Stacy sighed. She didn't like eating Pop-Tarts for breakfast; they just never felt enough. Yet, she had no choice today.

Stacy ran out of the house at top speed, munching on the Pop-Tart as she made her way to the bus stop. It seemed lady luck had simply abandoned her this morning. Stacy was just a half mile from the bus stop when she saw the last student climb onto the school bus. The door to the bus closed, and the bus driver drove off.

"No, no, no!" Stacy cried. "Stop!"

It was no use; the bus had already left. Not only would she be late for school, but walking all the way meant she would miss most of the first period, too. Her first lesson was English, a subject she was good at. All weekend, she had worked on writing the perfect piece of fiction. A masterpiece she had been waiting to show to her teacher. Now, she wouldn't be able to.

Half of the first lesson had passed by the time she reached school. As she entered class, she could feel the scrutinizing gaze of her classmates poking into her back. The most painful reaction was that of Mrs. Johnson. She looked disappointed. An expression that had never been directed at Stacy.

Stacy didn't get the opportunity to explain herself. Mrs. Johnson wordlessly extended the tardy slip to her. Stacy felt so embarrassed she could barely mutter an apology before she left to take her seat.

For Stacy, things just got worse and worse.

The next lesson was math. A subject Stacy didn't excel at. Just doing a normal classwork exercise was a chore, but today, it came with a bomb. Their teacher, Mr. Peter, had taken a pop quiz last week.

As he gave the day's assignment to them, he announced, "I've checked your quizzes and will distribute them shortly."

Stacy knew he hadn't done well on the quiz. Yet, when Mr. Peter slapped her quiz paper on her desk, a shocked gasp escaped her lips.

"This can't be?!" Stacy said in disbelief as she stared at the giant red "F" on her paper.

She had failed.

"Ms. Stacy," Mr. Johnson called. "Can I please have a word?" He said as he sat back at his desk.

As Stacy shuffled to the front of the class, she knew what Mr. Peter would say.

"Ms. Stacy, I'm very disappointed with your performance," he said.

At that moment, Stacy wanted to burst into tears. Her day hadn't started well; she didn't get to enjoy her favorite subject, and now she had failed math. She had never failed a subject, ever. Before Mr. Peter could say anything more, the bell rang, signaling the end of the period.

As the tide of students flooded out of the class, Stacy allowed herself to be pushed out with them—anything to save herself from further embarrassment.

It was finally Stacy's lunch period. She needed to let out the emotions swirling inside of her. And what better way to do that than to talk to her best friends?

Even that didn't go as planned.

"…and then she called Jake," Sylvie went on.

"I…" Stacy had just started to say something when she was cut off.

"We have to tell Tracy," Maria commented.

"I …" Stacy tried again.

And again

And again.

But somehow, her friends always ignored her voice. It seemed they were just so busy with their own stories and problems that they didn't care to know what was happening with her.

"I can't stay here," Stacy thought.

More than anything she had faced that day, it hurt that none of her friends had time for her. Stacy could feel tears pooling in her eyes. She couldn't take the embarrassment of being a crybaby, not after the awful day she had.

Silently, Stacy got up and left the cafeteria. She found a secluded corner in the school garden. That's when the floodgates opened. She cried and cried and cried.

Through her tears, she failed to notice someone passing by.

"Hey," a voice called out. "Are you okay?".

Stacy blinked through the flood of tears to see who it was. She saw ruffled blond hair, a freckled face, and brown eyes hidden behind round spectacles. It was none other than Tom McKay.

Tom was a boy in Stacy's science class. Although they had been studying together for almost a year, this was the first time he talked to her. Tom was a brilliant student who always sat in front of the class and answered all the teacher's questions. If he weren't in class, you'd probably find him working on one of his numerous experiments in the lab. Stacy was the total opposite. She was more of a social butterfly who loved organizing and being part of significant school events.

"Is everything all right?" Tom repeated his question as Stacy continued to stare at him silently.

Stacy quickly wiped her eyes. "I'm fine; it's just my pollen allergy acting up."

Tom blinked at her, not believing a word. "That's one wild allergy you have." He sat beside her and asked again, "For real, what's wrong? You can tell me; maybe I can help you?"

His expression was so sincere that Stacy felt like pouring out all her problems to him for a moment. But then, the doubts crept in.

What if he laughs at my problems?

What if he thinks I'm just being silly?

The list of "What ifs" was never-ending. But, for some reason, Stacy wanted to free herself of doubts. So, without thinking, she told Tom everything. At first, Stacy felt like crying again as she relived the painful events of the day. Yet, as she continued speaking, she felt lighter and lighter.

A heavy weight pressing down on her soul, crushing her spirit under it, started to lift.

Tom carefully listened to all Stacy had to say, not interrupting her.

"That's horrible," Tom said. "I wish I could've helped you."

As Tom said those words, Stacy realized something. Tom was wrong. He had already helped her in the best way possible.

"You already have," Stacy replied with a soft smile. "Sometimes all a person needs is a listening ear."

EPILOGUE

-cue the drum roll-

Celebrations are in order because you, my champion, have completed one milestone in our journey. You've finished this book.

By now, I sincerely hope each of these stories has helped you grow and helped to remind you of a fact I always knew to be true: you are Awesome!

Through the tales of each girl in this book, I hope you'll see that you are never alone in your struggles. And no matter how tough times are, YOU can make your way out. And as you shine at your brightest, in the darkest hours, you become a ray of hope for all those around you.

At the end of this book, if there is one thing I'd like to say, it's that I know you have the power to do it all. You can be the hero of your own story. And know I will be cheering for you every step of the way. Know that I am proud of who you are. Maybe one day, you'll want to share your story with the rest of the world, too.

Until then, thank you for becoming a part of this book! Your next milestone will be to become your own hero. I'll be cheering for you, supergirl!

Your biggest fan and supporter

Michelle

REVIW

As a children's book author, it would not only be a great help but also a joy for me if you could leave an honest review on Amazon.

I believe that these types of books play a crucial role in nurturing children's character, boosting their self-confidence, enhancing their relationships with friends and family, and encouraging them to be the best version of themselves, all while bringing them happiness.

I hope we can share many more stories together!

Here's the QR code for the review. Choose the marketplace of your preferred country!

Amazon US review	Amazon UK review	Amazon Canada review

Made in the USA
Las Vegas, NV
24 February 2024